CHAMPIONS FOR GOD

JERRY FALWELL

CHAMPIONS FOR GOD

While this book is designed for the reader's personal enjoyment and profit, it is also intended for group study. A Leader's Guide with Victor Multiuse Transparency Masters is available from your local bookstore or from the publisher.

VICTOR

BOOKS a division of SP Publications, Inc.
WHEATON. ILLINOIS 60187

Offices also in
Whitby, Ontario, Canada
Amersham-on-the-Hill, Bucks, England

Scripture quotations are from the *King James Version*.

Recommended Dewey Decimal Classification: 248
Suggested Subject Heading: Bible—Biography

Library of Congress Catalog Card Number: 85-50311
ISBN: 0-89693-534-5

VICTOR BOOKS
A division of SP Publications, Inc.
          Wheaton, Illinois 60187

CONTENTS

ACKNOWLEDGMENT

I am deeply indebted to Ed Hindson and Harold Willmington for their assistance in editing my sermons on "Twelve Champions," from which the text of this book was taken.

Recognition is also due to Mrs. Jeanne Mason and Mrs. Marilyn Temple who typed the original manuscript.

To
DR. B.R. LAKIN
that great champion of God
and the 20th century's
"Prince of Preachers"

SURROUND YOURSELVES WITH CHAMPIONS

GOD does not want us to be anything less than champions. God never calls any of us to be quitters or losers. He calls us to be winners and conquerors through Jesus Christ. But becoming a real champion requires discipline—for true champions are made, not born.

Many lessons must be learned if we are going to be champions. One crucial lesson is that we must surround ourselves with those who will challenge us to do our best.

David surrounded himself with 30 mighty men who had outstanding abilities and talents. These men were dedicated to their task and to David. They fought for David, and some gave their lives in battle. Three of the men fought just to get their commander a drink of water. With his friends' help, David became an effective military conqueror and a great king. He became a champion by surrounding himself with champions.

Jesus our Lord did not begin His ministry with several thousand followers. He selected 12 men who became champions. One later defaulted, but the 11 who remained later turned the world upside down.

The Apostle Paul surrounded himself with champions. One

was Barnabas, who accompanied Paul on his first missionary journey. Another was Titus, who had a specialized ministry of nurturing and building up the local churches Paul had planted.

Paul, writing from the Roman prison where he later died, told Timothy, "The time of my departure is at hand" (2 Tim. 4:6). He challenged Timothy to carry on his work. "And the things that thou hast heard of me among many witnesses, the same commit thou to faithful men, who shall be able to teach others also" (2:2). Timothy was commanded to do what Paul had done—to gather around him young champions, to teach them, train them, and communicate his message and soul-winning zeal to them. The ultimate characteristic of a champion is that he have a "Timothy."

God wants you to be a champion. If you're going to be a Sunday School teacher, a bus captain, a pastor, an evangelist, or a musician—be the best. God wants you to be an overcomer who attains the very best you can for His glory.

As you go about your work for God, you will have opposition. But champions are made in adversity. Bad days, problems, heartaches, and losses are all necessary elements in molding champions. God blesses stability. From time to time, your world may collapse around you, but that is when God is trying to teach you. Stability is born in the storm. It is not born in prosperity; it is born in adversity. You can only learn strength when you are in trouble. Learning to handle the opposition will make you a champion.

If you're going to be a champion, you must learn to multiply yourself by *training others*. A real champion does not try to do everything himself. A champion knows how to function as part of a team.

I've always been a fan of the New York Yankees. I remember when Mickey Mantle, Bobby Richardson, Elston Howard, and a host of others knew how to win ballgames. Though Mickey Mantle got most of the credit and a lot of the fame, the Yankees' success was a result of teamwork.

A champion is not an individual star, but a team player who knows how to function with others. The work of a local church has to be the work of a team composed of champions. Men and women of God are interested in learning all they can, mastering all the skills they can, acquiring all the maturity possible for the Lord Jesus, and then manifesting, teaching, and committing to others what they have learned.

The Apostle Paul told Timothy, "Thou therefore endure hardness, as a good soldier of Jesus Christ" (2 Tim. 2:3). From his prison cell, Paul wrote, "All my friends have gone, only Luke is with me" (see 2 Tim. 4:11). Yet in that lonely, filthy dungeon, Paul said, "Timothy, I want you to know if you're going to be a champion, you've got to pay the price."

What is the price of being a great Christian? When you got saved, you probably thought everyone would pat you on the back and tell you, "Boy, you're a great guy." You went back to work; and instead of your friends cheering you and praising you, they laughed, criticized you, and whispered about you behind your back. Your critics said, "It won't last, he'll fall; I'll give him three weeks." At home, you thought surely everybody in your family would be glad. But they said, "Don't become a religious fool. It's one thing to be a good churchman, but you don't have to go to the extreme." You found opposition from everybody everywhere. Opposition is part of the hardness you have to endure.

Champions *endure hardness* as good soldiers of Jesus Christ. Your tithe is the Lord's. Your time is the Lord's. Your talent is the Lord's. Satan, the world, and the flesh are all against you (1 John 2:16-17). All want to keep you from being a champion. But no matter what, you must live above the pressure. Joshua said, "As for me and my house, we will serve the Lord" (Joshua 24:15). Make that same commitment in your heart and don't ever turn back.

If you are going to be a champion, you must be *single-minded in your purpose.* A good soldier does not run off on tangents. He does not get involved in things which may hinder him from being a champion. The one common denominator of great men of God is that they had one single purpose and never veered from it. They were not sidetracked by fame or fortune. Their business was serving God constantly. Nothing interfered. Whatever God has called you to do for Him, do it with all your heart.

A champion must *learn to live by the rules.* If you expect God's blessings upon your life, you must live by God's blueprint. God has a perfect will for every life. You are only going to be a champion if you accept God's will, get in it, and do it.

The difference between a champion and a defeated Christian is usually a very small thing. Sometimes, it is just a little habit. Perhaps the defeated Christian never saw why he needed to study his Bible everyday or why he needed to spend time in prayer. Maybe he never saw why his clothes, his demeanor, his lifestyle, and his testimony had to be disciplined and decent. But a champion obeys all the rules. A champion finds out what God wants and—no matter how demanding, how strict, how disciplinary—he responds, "Lord, here am I, send me, use me."

D.L. Moody, early in his Christian life, heard a preacher say, "It yet remains to be seen what God can do with one man who is wholly surrendered to the Lord." Moody left that building saying in his heart, "By God's grace, I'll be that man." He shook two continents for God in his day. I wonder what God could do with a church, a corporate body of believers, who commit themselves to being champions for Christ. I believe we could shake the world for God.

Why do we need to surround ourselves with champions? The Bible teaches that a person usually becomes like those with whom he associates. We should fellowship with champions because they conform us to championship status. "A company of fools will be destroyed, while a man that walks with wise men shall be wise." Being around godly men makes one godly. Being around spiritual men makes one spiritual. The opposite is likewise true.

We should also surround ourselves with champions for the purpose of *competition*. Any athlete knows he performs better against stiff competition. When a runner is competing against someone who is not very fast, he seldom sets a record. Why? Because he is not driving to excel. We need around us, not world conformists, but men and women conformed to Christ, men and women who aspire to be like Jesus.

Surround yourselves with those who live the life of faith, those who think big things for God. Surround yourselves with people who are victorious; soul-winners who desire to capture this world for Christ. That kind of competition will force you to trust God for bigger and better things.

Surround yourselves with champions for *protection*. This is not physical protection, but spiritual immunization from the world, the flesh, and the devil. We need men and women who will shield us from the influence of carnality and worldliness. If you run with the crowd that tells dirty jokes or occasionally goes to the wrong places, soon your shields will be down. But if you get around godly people who pray about everything, you will find yourself protected.

How does a Christian surround himself with champions? First, he must begin in the *home*. A dad's first requirement is to build a family of champions. He must see that Jesus Christ is preeminent in the home, and that love and character-building are taught there.

Beyond the home, a Bible-believing, soul-winning *local church* is necessary to build and maintain champions. Every Christian needs to be part of a New Testament church where he can identify with God's people.

A *Christian school* is another way to surround your children with champions. It will cost. But if you will put your sons and daughters under saved school teachers, you will raise up champions.

Surround yourselves with champions by reading great *books*. Of course, the Bible is the greatest of all books. But biographies of great men, like C.T. Studd, Adoniram Judson,

Evan Roberts, and Charles Spurgeon can also motivate you.

Surround yourselves with the many champions of the Bible. In the chapters that follow, you will be introduced to 12 of the greatest champions of God. Let the principles that made them great mold and shape your life.

You too can be a champion for God!

ONE
ABRAHAM, THE FAITHFUL

NAME: Abraham, "father of a multitude"
DATES: 2165—1990 B.C.
CHARACTER QUALITY: Faithfulness
SIGNIFICANCE: Father of both Arabs
and Jews; progenitor of the line of the
Messiah and spiritual father of all believers
KEY TEXT: Genesis 11:27—12:5

ABRAHAM was raised in the ancient city of Ur and did not come to know God until he was 75 years old (Gen. 12:1, 4). Called out of paganism into fellowship with the true and living God, Abraham stands as the ultimate human example of faith in God. In spite of his personal limitations and failures, he emerged as a pillar of confidence in the promises of God. Against all odds, he believed God for the impossible and saw it become reality.

Abraham was a man who had nothing, yet believed God for everything. He became one of the most influential men of his day because of his faith in God. We, like him, need to trust God for the impossible. We need to learn to exercise our faith in God. In spite of all our mistakes, shortcomings, and weaknesses, if we can learn to live by faith, we can overcome everything else. Come share the adventure as we examine the life of this great man of faith.

Abraham's Calling
Abraham stands as one of the most prominent figures in all of Scripture. He is mentioned over 300 times in the Bible, 234

times in the Old Testament and 74 times in the New Testament. Sixteen Old Testament books and eleven New Testament books refer to Abraham. He is the forefather of both the Arab and Jewish peoples and is described in Scripture as the father of all who put their faith in God (Rom. 4:16).

Abraham was born in Ur, a magnificent city of Babylon which was a seaport on the Persian Gulf. It was one of the most spectacular cities of the ancient world. We do not know a great deal about Abraham's early life or what even led to his conversion. In Acts 7:2, Stephen tells us, "The God of glory appeared unto our father Abraham, when he was in Mesopotamia." His original name, Abram, meant "great father." His name was later changed by God to Abraham, "father of a multitude" (Gen. 17:5).

"Now the Lord had said unto Abram, 'Get thee out of thy country, and from thy kindred, and from thy father's house, unto a land that I will show thee' " (Gen. 12:1). Instead of leaving his father, Abraham took his father Terah (meaning "loiterer" or "delay") with him and stopped in Haran some 700 miles northwest of Ur (11:31). Only after his father died did Abraham move on into the land of Canaan.

Like many of us, Abraham failed at first to completely obey God's call. Faith and discouragement are opposites. Faith means taking God at His Word no matter how bleak the circumstances appear to be. Discouragement and procrastination come from focusing on our circumstances instead of focusing on God's power. If you know God wants you to do something, then get to it. Stop delaying and start trusting.

Abraham experienced the blessing of prosperity throughout his earthly life. God was with him in virtually every endeavor and the hand of God's blessings was continually evident upon his life. The fact that God promised to make of him a great nation resulted in the miracle of the nation of Israel. Who can explain this nation except by supernatural providence! For 4,000 years the miracle of the Jewish nation has been here on earth even though various nations and armies have attempted to destroy them. Israel stands today as a fulfillment of God's promises to Abraham. She is one of the great nations of the modern world.

The commission which Abraham received from God was sevenfold:

1. I will make of thee a great nation (Gen. 12:2).
2. I will bless thee (v. 2).
3. I will make thy name great (v. 2).
4. Thou shalt be a blessing (v. 2).
5. I will bless them that bless thee (v. 3).
6. I will curse him that curseth thee (v. 3).
7. In thee shall all families of the earth be blessed (v. 3).

God also promised to make Abraham's name great. It is clearly evident by the fact that nearly every Jewish child in the synagogue and every Sunday School child in church knows who Abraham was and what he did. His name is prominent not only in the Christian faith, but also among Jews and Moslems as well.

I believe that history proves that those who bless the Jewish people will in turn be blessed. By the same token, those who curse her shall fall under God's judgment. History is replete with examples of the Roman Caesars and fanatics like Hitler who dared to touch the people of God and fell under that curse. Ultimately, all families of the earth are blessed through Abraham because he is the progenitor of the line of the Messiah. It is through Abraham that Jesus Christ entered the stream of humanity.

The story of Abraham revolves around the centrality of the promise of God to him. The degree to which Abraham believed God's promise was the degree to which God blessed him. Like any great decision of life, there would come a time of testing and for Abraham this came quickly. Having arrived in the land God had promised to him, he built altars to the Lord at Shechem and at Bethel (12:7-8). But soon a severe famine threatened the land and in desperation Abraham took his family and moved on to Egypt.

Abram went down into Egypt to sojourn there, for the famine was grievous in the land. And it came to pass, when he was come near to enter into Egypt, that he said unto Sarai his wife, "Behold now, I know that thou art a fair woman to look upon; therefore it shall come to pass, when the Egyptians shall see thee, that they shall say, 'This is his wife;' and they will kill me, but they will save thee alive. Say, I pray thee, thou art my sister; that it may be well with me for thy sake; and my soul shall live because of thee."

And it came to pass, that, when Abram was come into Egypt, the Egyptians beheld the woman that she was very fair. The princes also of Pharaoh saw her, and commended her before Pharaoh; and the woman was taken into Pharaoh's house. And he entreated Abram well for her sake; and he had sheep, and oxen, and he asses, and menservants, and maidservants, and she asses, and camels.

And the Lord plagued Pharaoh and his house with great plagues because of Sarai, Abram's wife. And Pharaoh called Abram, and said, "What is this that thou hast done unto me? Why didst thou not tell me that she was thy wife? Why saidst thou, 'She is my sister'? So I might have taken her to me to wife; now therefore behold thy wife, take her, and go thy way" (Gen. 12:10-19).

It was during this time in Egypt that Abraham's faith was severely tested. His disobedience led to several tragic results:

1. He grieved the Lord and weakened his own faith, falling in the same manner again later (see Gen. 20:1-14).

2. He became a poor testimony to the unbelieving Pharaoh, before whom he should have been an example of faith and fidelity.

3. He became a poor testimony to his nephew Lot.

4. He apparently picked up Hagar, the Egyptian handmaid (16:3) who later would become his mistress and the mother of Ishmael, the father of the Arabs.

Thus, out of the temporary lapse would come eventually the great conflicts of the Middle East which have gone on for nearly 40 centuries!

Abraham's Character

Upon his return to Canaan, Abraham again worshiped the Lord at Bethel (Gen. 13:3-4). Then he and Lot agreed to divide their land.

> And Lot lifted up his eyes, and beheld all the plain of Jordan, that it was well watered everywhere, before the Lord destroyed Sodom and Gomorrah, even as the garden of the Lord, like the land of Egypt, as thou comest unto Zoar. Then Lot chose him all the plain of Jordan; and Lot journeyed east; and they separated themselves the one from the other. Abram dwelled in the land of Canaan (13:10-12).

A study of Abraham's character reveals that he was kind, brave, and courageous. When war broke out between the kings of the east and those of the Dead Sea area, Sodom fell and Lot was taken captive (14:11-12). Lot himself had already slipped desperately, for he had "pitched his tent toward Sodom" (13:12) then moved into Sodom (14:12). But Abraham had compassion for Lot and came to his rescue.

Abraham gathered an army of 318 trained servants and courageously battled the kings of the east (14:14-15). He was completely victorious. Abraham "brought back all the goods, and also brought again his brother Lot, and his goods, and the women also, and the people" (v. 16).

Upon his return from battle, Abraham was met by Melchizedek, the king of Salem (Jerusalem), who was also a priest
of God. Scripture is not clear regarding the identity of Melchizedek. Ancient Hebrew tradition considered him to be
Shem. Christian tradition has often taken him to be Christ.
Others argue that he was merely a human king who was a
priest of God. In any case, Melchizedek blessed Abraham and
in turn Abraham paid tithes of all that he had to him (vv. 18-
20). Again we see one of the great character qualities of
Abraham. He refused the materialistic offer of the ungodly
Bera, the King of Sodom, who wanted to split the loot with
him (vv. 21-24). Instead Abraham returned everything, and
on top of that he tithed unto the Lord.

Notice that tithing here clearly predates the Law of Moses
by some 400 years. Tithing was not something that was only
prescribed in the Mosaic Law and disappeared with the period
of grace, but has been practiced by the people of God
throughout history. It was demanded by the Law. But the
spirit of the New Testament is to go beyond the letter of the
Law and fulfill the intent of the Law. New Testament Christian giving ought to be over and above the minimum of the
tithe (Mark 12:41-44; 2 Cor. 9:7). When someone uses the
excuse that they do not believe in the legalism of tithing, you
can be certain that they do not believe in the cheerfulness of
giving either!

God's Covenant with Abraham

The turning point in Abraham's life comes in Genesis 15.
Having gone childless for years, Abraham suggests that he
might adopt his servant, Eliezer, as an heir (v. 5). However,
God promises to give Abraham a descendant of his own: "He
that shall come forth out of thine own bowels shall be thine
heir" (v. 4).

The Bible tells us that Abraham "believed in the Lord; and
He counted it unto him for righteousness" (v. 6). It is this

responsive belief that the New Testament states is the means
of our salvation (John 1:7; 14:1; 20:31). The basis of salvation has always been the grace of God (Rom. 3:24; Eph. 2:5,
8). The means of our salvation is faith in God (Mark 5:36).
Abraham is the first man recorded in Scripture to believe
God. This does not mean that he was the first believer, rather
that his faith is a pattern for all future believers. Notice that
Abraham did not please God, but he *believed* in God.

The New Testament illustrates this by the concept of
imputation. Adam's sin was imputed to the human race
(Rom. 3:23; 5:12); our sin was imputed to Christ (1 Peter
2:24); then His righteousness was imputed to us (Rom. 5:16-
17; Gal. 3:6).

In response to God's promise, Abraham "cut" a covenant
with God. "Take Me an heifer of three years old, and a she
goat of three years old, and a ram of three years old, and a
turtledove, and a young pigeon. And [Abraham] took unto
him all these, and divided them in the midst, and laid each
piece one against another; but the birds divided he not"
(Gen. 15:9-10).

Abraham literally cut several animals in half and laid them
side by side, allowing a pathway between the pieces. In
ancient times when two people cut a covenant, they would
join hands and walk together between the pieces of the
animals. The purpose of this was to illustrate that half the
covenant was useless. You cannot get milk from half a cow,
especially if you have the wrong half!

But in this instance God did *not* come down and join hands
with Abraham and walk between the pieces. Instead, God
imposed a supernatural sleep upon Abraham, who lay help-
less, while God alone, in the representation of fire, moved
down between the pieces of the animals. "When the sun went
down, and it was dark, behold a smoking furnace, and a
burning lamp that passed between those pieces" (v. 17). This
indicated that God had established an unconditional covenant with Abraham.

A conditional covenant is dependent upon both parties meeting the conditions of the agreement. An unconditional covenant is determined by one party deciding to bless the other. Scripture beautifully illustrates that God has given us the unconditional covenant of salvation (Rom. 6:23; 8:1) and as well gives us the conditional terms of the blessings of that salvation (Rom. 6:16; 1 Cor. 9:24-25; James 1:12). When we accept God's free gift of eternal life, then we are on our way to heaven unconditionally—saved by faith! (Eph. 2:8-9) However, the degree to which we are blessed along the way depends on our obedience to Christ.

The Abrahamic covenant was sealed with a sevenfold prophecy which has already been fulfilled:

1. Abraham's descendants would be strangers in a foreign land (Gen. 15:13; Ex. 1:17).

2. Abraham's descendants would be servants in that land (Gen. 15:13; Ex. 1:10).

3. Their servitude would last some 400 years (Gen. 15:13; Ex. 12:40).

4. God would judge the nation which enslaved Israel (Gen. 15:14; Ex. 12:12, 29-30; 14:18, 21-31).

5. Abraham himself would not live to see this (Gen. 15:15; 25:8).

6. After four long generations in bondage, Israel would return to the Promised Land (Gen. 15:16; Ex. 12:40-41).

7. Israel would come out of Egypt with great substance (Gen. 15:14; Ex. 12:35-38).

Abraham's Compromise
As time passed Abraham still did not have a descendant. Finally his wife Sarai persuaded him that what God meant was that *he* would have a child, but that *she* would not. She suggested that they follow the pagan custom of having a child

by the wife's handmaid, Hagar. The slave girl would thereby serve as a surrogate mother.

Abraham gave in to Sarai's pleading and the child which was eventually born was Ishmael, the forefather of the Arab people. Because of family tensions between the two women, Hagar was eventually dismissed.

All of this caused tremendous personal tragedy in Abraham's life as well as ongoing agony for the Arab and Jewish peoples until this day. Even though Ishmael, the father of the Arabs, was born 14 years before Isaac, the father of the Jews, God still promised the land to Isaac's descendants, not to Ishmael's descendants. This is a very important factor in the Jewish-Arab debate over the Palestinian issue. While the Arabs certainly have a right to *live* in the land, Israel has the God-given right to *rule* the land.

Abraham's Circumcision

As Genesis 16 ends, Abraham is at the lowest spiritual point of his life. He is out of fellowship with God and his family. He is no longer an effective leader; everything has apparently gone wrong. He was 86 years old when Ishmael was born; for the next 13 years there was no recorded message from God to Abraham. However, the gracious forgiving God speaks to him when he is 99 and tells him, "I will make My covenant between Me and thee, and will multiply thee exceedingly . . . . Thou shalt be a father of many nations. Neither shall thy name anymore be called Abram, but thy name shall be Abraham; for a father of many nations have I made thee. And I will make thee exceeding fruitful, and I will make nations of thee, and kings shall come out of thee" (Gen. 17:2, 4-6).

In the context of Abraham's time, this must have seemed ludicrous. Here is a man whose name meant "father of many" who for 85 years was a father of none! Now at 99 having only one son, by his wife's handmaid, his name is changed to "father of a multitude"! Again God reaffirmed His covenant with Abraham and promised to give him the land and to secure it to his seed (v. 8). The rite of circumcision was instituted as a sign of God's promise. Even his wife's name, Sarai ("contentious") was changed to Sarah ("princess"). Their name changes indicate that this was a great turning point in their lives.

The sign of circumcision indicated that all of Abraham's offspring were uniquely dedicated unto God. Today, we know of the health benefits of this practice as well. God literally was marking His people in a unique way to indicate that they belonged to Him. The New Testament explains that circumcision alone did not save anyone, but that it was an outward sign of God's covenant with Israel (Rom. 2:25-29; 1 Cor. 7:18-19).

Abraham's Compassion

> And the Lord said, "Shall I hide from Abraham that thing which I do; seeing that Abraham shall surely become a great and mighty nation. . . . Because the cry of Sodom and Gomorrah is great, and because their sin is very grievous; I will go down now, and see whether they have done altogether according to the cry of it, which is come unto Me; and if not, I will know" (Gen. 18:17-18, 20-21).

In spite of the wickedness of Sodom and Gomorrah and Lot's foolish decision to move there, Abraham pleaded with God to spare these cities. In typical Near Eastern bargaining style, Abraham began by asking God to spare the cities if 50 righteous persons might be found there (v. 24). He then lowered the request to 45, then 40, 30, 20, and finally 10 (vv. 28-32). Underestimating human depravity, Abraham stopped with that figure. He believed that there would surely be at least 10 righteous people in Sodom and Gomorrah.

However, Scripture indicates that there was only one righteous person there—Lot! (2 Peter 2:7-8) The judgment of God which fell upon these cities is clearly described in Scripture. The Lord "rained upon Sodom and upon Gomorrah brimstone and fire from the Lord out of heaven" (Gen. 19:24). The cause of this judgment was homosexuality (vv. 4-10).

Because of Lot's willingness to live in the midst of all this moral corruption, he was unable to convince his sons-in-law to flee (v. 14). He also lost his wife, who kept lingering behind (v. 26). Lot finally ended up in an incestuous relationship with his own daughters (vv. 30-38). In spite of all this, Abraham genuinely cared about Lot and the souls of the people in wicked Sodom and Gomorrah. It is one thing for us to condemn and judge sin; it is quite a different matter to genuinely love the sinner.

I have often been criticized for my strong stand against homosexuality. I believe the Bible clearly teaches that this is a sin and deserving of God's judgment (Rom. 1:26-28). However, I have great compassion for homosexuals. Nothing would delight me more than to see homosexuals come to Christ, who alone can set them free. Abraham was truly God's champion because he was not only a man of faith and courage, but a man of compassion and kindness as well.

Abraham's Celebration

Abraham's life reaches its greatest climax with the birth of Isaac, whose name literally means "laughter." All of Abraham's life had been lived by faith that this day would become a reality. Abraham was 100 years old when the son of promise was finally born (Gen. 21:5). A great celebration was held to mark the time of the weaning of Isaac, probably at about age 3 (v. 8).

Ever since he left behind the pagan worship of the gods of Ur, Abraham believed that the true God would fulfill His promise to him. In the 25 years since he had left Haran, in spite of personal struggles, failures, and successes, Abraham looked forward to the day when God would give him the son of promise.

As the years rolled by, God called Abraham to take his son and offer him as a burnt offering upon Mount Moriah. "Take now thy son Isaac, whom thou lovest, and get thee into the land of Moriah; and offer him there for a burnt offering upon one of the mountains which I will tell thee of " (22:2).

This request was seemingly against the very nature of God Himself. But it was designed to increase Abraham's faith rather than destroy it. Child sacrifice is clearly outlawed in Scripture (Ex. 20:13; Lev. 18:21). Nevertheless, God asked Abraham to take the son of promise and sacrifice him back to the Promiser. God was testing to see whether Abraham's confidence was in the Promiser or in the promise.

Now having been matured by the tests of time, Abraham moved in complete obedience to the most incredible demand that God could ever make. He took Isaac to Mount Moriah (in the very area where the temple later would stand) and prepared to sacrifice him. However, Abraham told the servants, "Abide ye here with the ass; and I and the lad will go yonder and worship, and come again to you" (Gen. 22:5). Here we see evidence of Abraham's faith. He either believed that God would raise the boy from the dead, or that somehow God would provide a sacrifice in Isaac's place.

Isaac was now nearly 20 years old and fully capable of resisting his father. Isaac becomes a beautiful picture of Christ the Son willingly bound by the Father on the altar of sacrifice. However, as Abraham raises the knife, with every intention to obey God's command, the Angel of the Lord (Christ Himself) calls to him from heaven.

> "Lay not thine hand upon the lad, neither do thou any thing unto him; for now I know that thou fearest God, seeing thou hast not withheld thy son, thine only son from Me."

And Abraham lifted up his eyes, and looked,
and behold behind him a ram caught in a thicket
by his horns; and Abraham went and took the ram
and offered him up for a burnt offering in the stead
of his son (Gen. 22:12-13).

The test has been passed and the ram caught in the thicket
becomes the sacrifice in Isaac's place. Thus, Abraham named
the altar Jehovah-jireh ("the Lord provides"). What God
would not allow Abraham to do in sacrificing his son, our
heavenly Father did on our behalf when He gave His Son to
die for our sins.

Conclusion

This incident on Mount Moriah was the epitome of Abraham's faith in God. It reveals why he was a true champion of
God. His years of believing God's promise were tested in a
moment of great personal agony. The result was a resounding
triumph of the grace of God—"God provides!"

As we look at the life of Abraham, we see that where God
guides, He provides. Through the difficult circumstances of
his life, God taught Abraham the lesson of faith in the wise
and gracious provision of an all-loving God. How much we
too need to trust Him in our daily walk as believers.

I have spent a lifetime helping people with problems. Time
and time again I have seen God do the impossible for those
who believed all hope was gone. Don't give up on God. Just
when you need Him most He will be there to meet your need.

Many of our students at Liberty Baptist College have testified year after year how God has met their financial needs. I
remember a young man who believed God would provide him
with a van for his ministry. He even believed it would come
before Christmas. When school let out that semester for the
Christmas break he went home without the van. He still
trusted God to meet his need, but he began to wonder if he
had asked for too much. When he arrived home, someone

gave him a brand new vehicle just before Christmas. God had met his need just in time. Today, that young man is pastoring a church and serving the Lord.

God will never put more on you than He puts in you to bear it up. When you think you have trusted God all you can; you have prayed all you know how; you have cried the last teardrops; you are about to give up; you have no more strength left in you; God will step in and pump new life into you (Isa. 40:31). He will meet your need in your most desperate hour. Trust Him!

TWO
MOSES, THE LAWGIVER

NAME: Moses, "drawn out of water"
DATES: 1525—1405 B.C.
CHARACTER QUALITY: Endurance
SIGNIFICANCE: Author of the Pentateuch;
    leader of the Exodus; giver of God's Law
KEY TEXT: Hebrews 11:24-26

MOSES was one of the most important men in the Old Testament. Through his leadership, the nation of Israel was delivered from Egypt and brought to the edge of the Promised Land. Rescued and saved from drowning and starvation by Pharaoh's daughter, Moses was raised as royalty in Egypt. Educated, talented, and brilliant, the Prince of Egypt refused to be called the son of Pharaoh's daughter and chose rather to suffer with the people of God.

D.L. Moody once said, "Moses spent the first 40 years of his life trying to be somebody, the next 40 years realizing he was a nobody, and the final 40 years, under God, helping everybody!" It was during his years of obscurity that Moses learned the endurance that would enable him to stand against the king of the greatest nation in the world.

Prince of Egypt: The First 40 Years

Moses was born about 1525 B.C. His parents were from the tribe of Levi and were slaves in Egypt where the Israelites had been in bondage for nearly 400 years. Moses was the youngest of three children, his sister Miriam being the oldest and

Aaron being the next oldest in the family. Moses was born during a time of persecution when the Egyptian Pharaoh was determined to exterminate all newborn Hebrew male children. When Moses was only three months old, his mother

> took for him an ark of bulrushes, and daubed it with slime and with pitch, and put the child therein; and she laid it in the flags by the river's brink. And his sister stood afar off, to wit what would be done to him. And the daughter of Pharaoh came down to wash herself at the river; and her maidens walked along by the river's side; and when she saw the ark among the flags, she sent her maid to fetch it. And when she had opened it, she saw the child; and, behold, the babe wept. And she had compassion on him, and said, "This is one of the Hebrews' children."
>
> Then said his sister to Pharaoh's daughter, "Shall I go and call to thee a nurse of the Hebrew women, that she may nurse the child for thee?"
>
> And Pharaoh's daughter said to her, "Go."
>
> And the maid went and called the child's mother.
>
> And Pharaoh's daughter said unto her, "Take this child away, and nurse it for me, and I will give thee thy wages."
>
> And the woman took the child, and nursed it. And the child grew, and she brought him unto Pharaoh's daughter, and he became her son. And she called his name Moses; and she said, "Because I drew him out of the water" (Ex. 2:3-10).

Since all physical life in Egypt depends upon the waters of the Nile River, the Egyptians literally worshiped the river as a god. Believing the child to be a gift from the Nile River god, Pharaoh's daughter raised him as her son with every intention that he would one day reign as Pharaoh.

Moses was raised and educated in the palace as royalty. He

received the finest things that the world of his day could offer. His birth as a slave was virtually forgotten and he was considered a full-fledged Egyptian. During this time, Egypt reached one of its greatest heights of splendor and prosperity. Thus, Moses had every reason to deny his Hebrew heritage and live in luxury and ease. According to the New Testament, Moses was a very handsome man and an impressive leader (Acts 7:20; Heb. 11:23). He was also an educated and talented man (Acts 7:22) who was "learned in all the wisdom of the Egyptians" and "mighty in words and in deeds."

However, the early years of Moses' life came to a tragic end. Unable to deny his compassion for the Hebrew slaves, Moses killed an Egyptian who was severely beating one of the Hebrews. Moses then hid the body in the sand, assuming that no one would ever find out what he had done.

> And when [Moses] went out the second day, behold, two men of the Hebrews strove together; and he said to him that did the wrong, "Wherefore smitest thou thy fellow?"
>
> And he said, "Who made thee a prince and judge over us? Intendest thou to kill me, as thou killedst the Egyptian?"
>
> And Moses feared, and said, "Surely this thing is known."
>
> Now when Pharaoh heard this thing, he sought to slay Moses. But Moses fled from the face of Pharaoh, and dwelt in the land of Midian; and he sat down by a well (Ex. 2:13-15).

Falling under the indictment of Pharaoh, Moses fled for his life, leaving behind the splendor of Egypt.

Shepherd of Midian: The Second 40 Years

The next period of Moses' life was spent in virtual isolation and obscurity in the land of Midian in the Sinai desert. There he met and married Zipporah, the daughter of Jethro (Ex.

2:21). What little we know of Moses' life during this time is recorded in Exodus 2—3. His father-in-law is described as "the priest of Midian" (2:16). It is possible that Jethro was a believer in the true God, though this is not made clear in the text.

The turning point of these days of anguish and obscurity came at the burning bush. "And the angel of the Lord appeared unto [Moses] in a flame of fire out of the midst of a bush; and he looked, and behold, the bush burned with fire, and the bush was not consumed. . . . And when the Lord saw that he turned aside to see, God called unto him out of the midst of the bush, and said, 'Moses, Moses.' And he said, 'Here am I' " (3:2, 4). Notice that Moses was at the height of his success when he fell into sin; and he was in the depths of obscurity when he was called of God to deliver Israel.

In a face to face revelation at the burning bush, God said to Moses, "Draw not nigh hither; put off thy shoes from thy feet, for the place whereon thou standest is holy ground. . . . I am the God of thy father, the God of Abraham, the God of Isaac, and the God of Jacob" (vv. 5-6). Scripture tells us that Moses was afraid and fell on his face before God. The Lord proceeded to tell Moses that He was aware of the affliction of his people.

> And I am come down to deliver them out of the hand of the Egyptians, and to bring them up out of that land unto a good land and a large, unto a land flowing with milk and honey; unto the place of the Canaanites, and the Hittites, and the Amorites, and the Perizzites, and the Hivites, and the Jebusites. . . . Come now therefore, and I will send thee unto Pharaoh, that thou mayest bring forth My people the Children of Israel out of Egypt (3:8, 10).

Having confronted Moses, God commissioned him to go to Pharaoh and demand freedom for the Children of Israel.

The conversation that ensued between God and Moses

clearly indicates God's personal concern and His willingness
to use fallible human beings to accomplish His will. Moses
protested that Pharaoh would not listen to him (3:11), and
that the Children of Israel would question his authority,
asking him to name the name of God (v. 13). God responded, "Thus shalt thou say unto the Children of Israel, 'I AM
hath sent me unto you.' And they shall hearken to thy voice;
and thou shalt come, thou and the elders of Israel, unto the
king of Egypt, and ye shall say unto him, 'The Lord God of
the Hebrews hath met with us; and now let us go, we beseech
thee, three days' journey into the wilderness, that we may
sacrifice to the Lord our God' " (vv. 14, 18). At the same
time, God warned Moses that the king of Egypt would not let
the Israelites go except through divine intervention (vv. 19-
20).

Moses did everything humanly possible to get out of this
divine appointment. He protested that he was not an adequate leader or speaker (4:10). To encourage him, God
promised, "Now therefore go, and I will be with thy mouth,
and teach thee what thou shalt say" (v. 12). This was a
promise of direct revelation from God to Moses as the instrument of receiving the Word of God.

Further, the Lord told Moses to throw his staff to the
ground. Moses obeyed, and his staff immediately became a
serpent. God then told him to pick it up by the tail (the worst
place you can pick up a snake) and it again became a rod.

As another sign, the Lord told Moses to put his hand in his
bosom and to take it out. When Moses obeyed, his hand was
covered with leprosy. God then told Moses to return his hand
to his bosom and pull it out again. When Moses did, his hand
was healed (vv. 6-8).

All of this was done to reduce Moses' reluctance to return
to Egypt and to build his faith in the power of the Lord.
Moses was not an illiterate shepherd. He was an intelligent
and highly educated man. But he had suffered a distressing
personal tragedy and embarrassment and was reluctant to

return to the place where he had failed. God used these miracles as signs that He could overrule any circumstance of life by His power.

Upon his return to Egypt, Moses was used of God to bring about the greatest confrontation between the true God and the gods of that age that had ever occurred. In Egyptian religion, the Pharaoh himself was literally considered to be a god; therefore, his son was considered to be "the son of god." Thus, the Lord instructed Moses, when you go before Pharaoh tell him, "Israel is My son, even My firstborn" (v. 22). The demand to release Israel from bondage was the demand of the true and living God to receive back His son from a false god, the Pharaoh of Egypt who had laid claim upon him.

There is no human way to explain the miraculous workings of God. He took a man of great skill, wisdom, and leadership and sent him into obscurity and oblivion in order to make him into a real leader of God's people.

Becoming a champion for God is a process. If we learn nothing else from the life of Moses, we should learn that success is never instantaneous in the will of God. From a human standpoint, it would appear that Moses wasted 40 years in the obscurity of the Midian desert. However, in the ultimate will of God, those were years of training and preparation. The "desert" years brought a maturity to Moses' life which could never have come in the splendor of Egypt. Thus, it was that his perspective on life drastically changed and he was prepared to refuse the wealth of Egypt for the reproach of Christ.

Lawgiver of God: The Third 40 Years

Moses' initial confrontation with Pharaoh led to disaster. Pharaoh rejected Moses' demands and made the Israelites' workload even more severe than it had already been (5:7-12). Even the Hebrew leaders complained and blamed Moses for their extra burdens (vv. 20-21).

However, the confrontation between Moses and Pharaoh was not merely on the human level. Rather, it was a confrontation of the true God with the false gods of Egypt. The ten plagues on the land of Egypt were designed not only to break Pharaoh's stubborn will, but to show the powerlessness of the Egyptian gods (Ex. 7—11).

PLAGUE	VS.	EGYPTIAN DEITY
1. Nile River turned to blood		1. River god *Nilus* and *Khunum*, guardian of the Nile
2. Millions of frogs		2. Sacred frog deity, *Heqt*, wife of *Khunum*
3. Swarms of lice (lit., gnats or beetles)		3. Sacred beetle scarabs good luck charms associated with the god *Kepera*
4. Swarms of flies		4. *Hatok*, the desert deity
5. Epidemic fever affecting cattle		5. *Apis*, the sacred bull and *Hathor*, the cow goddess
6. Boils on men and beasts		6. *Imhotep*, the god of medicine
7. Severe and destructive hail		7. *Shu* and *Qetesh*, nature's storm gods
8. Swarms of locusts		8. Moon goddess *Isis*, protector of Egypt
9. Thick darkness		9. *Ra*, the sun god
10. Death of the firstborn		10. *Ptah*, god of life and the deified Pharaoh himself

In all of this we see that Moses was merely the human instrument being used by God. Moses did not have the power to overcome the magnitude of Pharaoh or the multitude of Egypt, but the Lord Jehovah did. The plagues struck at the very basis of Egyptian society and left it in shambles.

But this was not the end of Moses' ministry. From that point, he led the Children of Israel through the wilderness to the edge of the Red Sea and there, by the mighty miracle of God, "Moses stretched out his hand over the sea; and the Lord caused the sea to go back by a strong east wind all that night, and made the sea dry land, and the waters were divided. And the Children of Israel went into the midst of the sea upon the dry ground; and the waters were a wall unto them on their right hand, and on their left" (14:21-22).

Eighty years earlier, Moses had floated helplessly as a babe on the waters of the Nile, but now he parts the waters of the mighty Red Sea!

Leading the reluctant Israelites through the Sinai wilderness, Moses was used of God to bring water from a rock and manna from heaven to meet the people's needs. He reinstituted the rite of circumcision and the observation of the Sabbath. He then went to Mount Sinai and received the Law directly from God Himself. It was summarized in the Ten Commandments (20:2-17):

1. Thou shalt have no other gods before Me (v. 3).
2. Thou shalt not make unto thee any graven image (v. 4).
3. Thou shalt not take the name of the Lord thy God in vain (v. 7).
4. Remember the Sabbath Day, to keep it holy (v. 8).
5. Honor thy father and thy mother (v. 12).
6. Thou shalt not kill (v. 13).
7. Thou shall not commit adultery (v. 14).
8. Thou shalt not steal (v. 15).

9. Thou shalt not bear false witness against thy neighbor (v. 16).
10. Thou shalt not covet (v. 17).

The first four commandments govern man's relationship to God; the remaining six govern our relationship to one another. In the final analysis, the prosperity of any nation is directly linked to that nation's observance of these Ten Commandments. They form the basis of the Judeo-Christian ethical system and are the foundation of law in all of western society. Thus, the blessing of God is determined in direct proportion to a nation's obedience to the laws of God. The psalmist reminds us, "The wicked shall be turned into hell, and nations that forget God" (Ps. 9:17).

Moses also built the tabernacle as a visible worship center for the people of Israel and a place to house the glory of God (Ex. 26—31). The tabernacle illustrates the overall plan of salvation:

1. There was only one doorway upon the altar before one could enter the presence of God.

2. A lamb had to be sacrificed upon the altar before one could enter the presence of God.

3. The brazen laver was there for continual cleansing from sin.

4. The lampstand (menorah) was there reminding us that Christ is the light of the world.

5. The shewbread was there reminding us that Christ is the bread of life.

6. The altar of incense was there reminding us of the importance of continual prayer.

Thus, the tabernacle and its symbolism was designed to point the Israelites to Christ, the true Messiah and the one way of salvation by faith.

Moses' training in Midian enabled him to endure the many hardships in the wilderness journey which finally brought the Israelites to the edge of the Promised Land. Before his death God commanded Moses, "Get thee up into this mountain

Abarim, unto Mount Nebo, which is in the land of Moab, that is over against Jericho; and behold the land of Canaan, which I give unto the Children of Israel for a possession" (Deut. 32:49).

However, Moses was denied entrance into the land "because ye trespassed against Me among the Children of Israel at the waters of Meribah-Kachesh, in the wilderness of Zin; because ye sanctified Me not in the midst of the Children of Israel. Yet thou shalt see the land before thee; but thou shalt not go thither unto the land which I give the Children of Israel" (vv. 51-52).

So Moses went up into the mountains and viewed the Promised Land. Moses "died there in the land of Moab, according to the word of the Lord. And He buried him in a valley in the land of Moab, over against Bethpeor; but no man knoweth of his sepulcher unto this day" (34:5-6). The final epitaph of Scripture states, "And there arose not a prophet since in Israel like unto Moses, whom the Lord knew face to face" (v. 10).

Conclusion

Moses became a champion for God, not because he was raised in Egypt's splendor, but because he learned obedience. However, like all the characters of Scripture, Moses was not perfect. His anger caused him to kill an Egyptian and later caused him to strike the rock out of frustration. He often questioned the intent of God's instructions and became frustrated with the squabbling people of Israel as he led them through their wilderness journey.

However, Moses was a man of unusual faith and determination who was willing to stand against the greatest nation of his day. He was courageous, yet sensitive. He was an enduring laborer, a virtual workaholic. He loved his people and never gave up on God. He learned that the greatest lesson of leadership is to train and prepare adequate followers who can carry on God's work in the next generation. The evidence of Moses' success was Joshua.

One principle of Scripture to which I have committed myself is the importance of training others. In 1971 when we began Liberty Baptist College, it was with the intention that we would train a generation of Christian leaders to meet the challenges of the next era. The Apostle Paul clearly gave this plan to young Timothy when he wrote, "And the things that thou hast heard of me among many witnesses, the same commit thou to faithful men, who shall be able to teach others also" (2 Tim. 2:2).

I am convinced that if we are going to reach the next generation for Christ we must train young people to follow our example. We must be the kind of leaders that God can use to represent the cause of Christ to our own generation in such a way that we prepare the next generation to follow Him as well. The example of pastors, parents, teachers, and leaders is essential if we are to pass on the truth of the Word of God to the next generation. Let us never be content with our own day and time. We must provide the leadership that will ensure a better world for our children and our grandchildren to come.

THREE
JOSHUA, THE SOLDIER

NAME: Joshua, "savior" or "deliverer"
DATES: 1400—1390 B.C.
CHARACTER QUALITY: Courage
SIGNIFICANCE: Successor to Moses and
    leader of the Israelite conquest of Canaan
KEY TEXT: Joshua 1:1-9

WE know very little of Joshua's early life except that he was born as an Israelite slave in Egypt. He is referred to in Scripture as the son of Nun (1 Chron. 7:27). The meaning of his father's name is uncertain in Hebrew, but it apparently refers to the Egyptian god of Nun. This may imply that Joshua's father had forsaken the worship of Jehovah in order to accommodate his Egyptian masters. If this is so, it makes Joshua's life all the more unique because he became such a devoted servant of Jehovah.

Joshua became a good leader by learning to be a good follower. By overcoming his early years in slavery, he reminds us that under God, no one is limited by his family, race, or social background. The key to spiritual success is our surrender to the Lord.

From these humble beginnings, God raised up the greatest warrior of Bible times—Joshua, the soldier.

A Servant to Moses
Having been released from bondage under the leadership of Moses and by the mighty power of God, Joshua journeyed

with the rest of the Israelites through the Red Sea and into the Sinai wilderness. There Joshua learned leadership under Moses in a position similar to that of an understudy. He functioned as a minister or servant and later as a military commander (Ex. 24:13; 33:11; 17:8-13). During these years as Joshua learned to be a good follower, God was developing in him the qualities of a great leader.

Later, Joshua was chosen as one of the 12 spies sent into Canaan (Num. 13:1-20). He and Caleb were the only faithful spies who brought back positive reports on the potential of the forthcoming invasion (14:6-8). The other 10 spies brought back negative reports and the majority of the people listened to them and refused to follow Moses into the Promised Land. In this case, the "minority report" was the correct one and the people suffered years of futility in the wilderness for failing to follow the advice of Joshua and Caleb.

Israel did not remain in the wilderness for 40 years because they were *lost*, but because they were under the judgment of God: "Surely there shall not one of these men of this evil generation see that good land, which I swore to give unto your fathers" (Deut. 1:35). Thus the entire adult population of Israel died in the wilderness during the next 40 years, except for Joshua and Caleb (vv. 29-38).

Therefore, Joshua was one of the few survivors of the entire journey. He had lived in Egypt as a slave, come out in the Exodus, survived the wilderness journey, and finally entered into the Promised Land. He and Caleb and the children who came out of Egypt in the original Exodus were the only slaves who lived to see the land possessed. The others who entered the Promised Land were those young people who had been born in the wilderness during the 40-year wandering (v. 39).

A Savior for Israel
Joshua's name is the Hebrew form of Jesus, meaning "savior." It was an appropriate name for the great warrior be-

cause he was indeed a deliverer of his people. He prefigured Christ in the sense that he brought victory to his people and delivered them into the land of promise. In that sense, he was a savior. Christ, by contrast, is our Saviour because He gives us salvation and delivers us into heaven.

God's promise of success does not come as a result of our abilities, but rather as a result of our commitment to His Word. One key to Joshua's success as a leader was his commitment to the Word of God. In the beginning of the conquest, God commanded Joshua:

> This book of the law shall not depart out of thy mouth; but thou shalt meditate therein day and night, that thou mayest observe to do according to all that is written therein; for then thou shalt make thy way prosperous and then thou shalt have good success. Have I not commanded thee? Be strong and of a good courage; be not afraid, neither be thou dismayed; for the Lord thy God is with thee whithersoever thou goest (Josh. 1:8-9).

Throughout his military career, Joshua was convinced that he had a mandate from God Himself. As he prepared to conquer Jericho, the Commander of the Lord's army appeared to Joshua, sword in hand, and gave him God's battle plan (5:13-15). It is almost certain that since the appearances of the Angel of the Lord in the Old Testament are references to Christ Himself that this is THE Saviour appearing to A savior.

As Joshua wondered how he could conquer Jericho, Christ appeared and gave him the answer. The battle plan consisted of carrying the ark of the covenant around the city once each day for six days and seven times on the seventh day. This was to be followed by the blowing of rams' horns and a shout and the promise that the city wall would fall down before them (6:1-5). All of this was done miraculously to encourage the army of Israel to the great task that lay ahead of them, namely the conquest of the entire land of Canaan.

Several instances early in Joshua's life indicate his preparation for the task to which God had called him. When the
Israelites arrived at the Jordan River, the Lord commanded
Joshua to have the priests carry the ark before the people into
the water which He promised would part, just as the Red Sea
had parted before Moses (3:1-17). God did this to magnify
Joshua before the people. This was God's vote of confidence
in Joshua's leadership: "This day I will begin to magnify you
in the sight of all Israel, that they may know that, as I was
with Moses, so I will be with you" (v. 7).

Having crossed the Jordan, Joshua reinstated the rite of
circumcision. No explanation is given in Scripture for why
the people who came out of Egypt and died in the wilderness
never circumcised their children who were born in the wilderness. But Joshua demanded that the entire army be circumcised before they moved on to Jericho. From a human standpoint, nothing could have been more ridiculous. However,
from the divine standpoint, nothing could have been more
appropriate.

A Military Leader

Joshua was a fearless fighter and a man of integrity. While
God used Moses to get the Israelites out of Egypt, He used
Joshua to get them into the Promised Land. Joshua had
learned to take orders from Moses and was thus ready to take
orders from God.

Joshua's military campaigns against the Canaanites can be
divided into three segments: central, southern, and northern
campaigns.

Central Campaign. Joshua's army crossed the Jordan River
near Jericho and set up its battle headquarters at Gilgal. From
there, they marched to Jericho, the major city of central
Canaan, and conquered it. The startling collapse of Jericho's
walls left the Canaanites in virtual shock. Jericho was over-
taken and burned to the ground by the Israelites.

However, this great victory was followed by the disgraceful defeat of Israel at Ai (meaning "ruin"), just a few miles from Jericho. This defeat was a direct result of one man's disobedience. "For Achan, the son of Carmi . . . took of the accursed thing; and the anger of the Lord was kindled against the Children of Israel" (Josh. 7:1). As a result of Achan's sin, the army fell under God's judgment and so did Achan (vv. 11-12, 20-21, 24-25).

The central campaign was followed by Joshua's only recorded mistake. The people of Gibeon, from a town a few miles north of Jerusalem, put on old clothes and pretended they had come on a long journey to make an alliance with Joshua. Scripture does not record that Joshua prayed or sought God's direction in this matter. He simply submitted to the alliance to save himself the trouble of having to conquer another town. Only later did he discover that rather than being from far away, the Gibeonites were really from the next major city over the hill (9:3-26). When news of the alliance spread, the Canaanite king of Jerusalem formed an alliance of his own to invade Gibeon and punish the Gibeonites for their cooperation with the Hebrews (10:3-5).

Southern Campaign. Because of the alliance he had made with the Gibeonites, Joshua came to their defense in the battle in the Valley of Ajalon. During this battle the sun stood still for an entire day (vv. 12-13). The kings of the south were eventually stopped at Makkedah when Joshua defeated an alliance representing the Canaanite cities of Jerusalem, Hebron, Jarmuth, Lachish, and Eglon. From that point, Joshua eventually took all the major cities of the southern area.

Northern Campaign. The northern Canaanite tribes quickly formed an alliance with the Amorites, Hittites, and Hivites (11:1-5). They rallied under the leadership of Jabin, king of Hazor. Like Lachish, Hazor was one of the largest and greatest of all of the Canaanite settlements. Extensive archeological excavations there have revealed that it was a major city with a population even greater than that of Jericho. The Bible tells us that Joshua defeated an alliance of the kings of Hazor, Madon, Shimron, and Achshaph in an overwhelming attack, chasing them all the way into what today is Lebanon. Then Joshua burned Hazor to the ground (v. 11). By the end of the northern campaign, the entire land was basically under Joshua's control. Joshua 12:7-24 records the 31 royal cities which Joshua conquered.

The theme for the Book of Joshua is *total victory*. Joshua paid the price for total victory and won every battle in which he fought. Even the temporary setback at Ai was quickly remedied. Joshua is the epitome of a victorious conqueror. Truly, he was one of God's greatest champions.

A Settler in the Land

Having conquered the land and driven out the majority of Israel's enemies, Joshua then turned his attention to dividing the land among the twelve tribes of Israel. The two tribes of Reuben and Gad and half of the tribe of Manasseh settled on the east side of the Jordan River, in what today is part of the nation of Jordan. The remaining tribes settled on the west bank of the Jordan River. The Book of Joshua gives a lengthy and detailed account of the boundaries, borders, and cities of these tribal settlements (Josh. 18:7—19:51). Scripture makes it clear that God's borders for Israel are even greater than that which she now possesses. In addition to allotting land to the twelve tribes, Joshua established cities of refuge and levitical cities for civil and priestly purposes (20:2—21:41).

Before his death, Joshua called together the elders and families of Israel and recounted the blessings of God upon their lives. He reminded them that God had fulfilled all that He had promised to do for them.

> And the Lord gave unto Israel all the land which
> He swore to give unto their fathers; and they
> possessed it, and dwelt therein. And the Lord gave

them rest round about, according to all that He
swore unto their fathers; and there stood not a man
of all their enemies before them; and the Lord
delivered all their enemies into their hand. There
failed not ought of any good thing which the Lord
had spoken unto the house of Israel; all came to
pass (21:43-45).

Joshua then challenged the Israelites to make a permanent
decision to follow the Lord:

Be ye therefore very courageous to keep and to do
all that is written in the book of the law of Moses,
that ye turn not aside therefrom to the right hand
or to the left; that ye come not among these
nations, these that remain among you; neither
make mention of the name of their gods, nor cause
to swear by them, neither serve them, nor bow
yourselves unto them; but cleave unto the Lord
your God, as ye have done unto this day (23:6-8).

The Canaanites at their borders would serve as a constant
snare to the Israelites' beliefs and convictions. Joshua urged
the Children of Israel to keep their enemies totally expelled
from the land. He reminded them that God had brought
them out of Egypt, through the Red Sea, across the wilderness, and into the land of promise which they now possessed.
Joshua ended his farewell address with these words:

And if it seem evil unto you to serve the Lord,
choose you this day whom ye will serve; whether
the gods which your fathers served that were on
the other side of the flood, or the gods of the
Amorites, in whose land ye dwell; but as for me
and my house, we will serve the Lord (24:15).

With this challenge, Joshua gave the people three
alternatives:

- They could go back to worshiping the gods of
  Babylon which their forefathers had worshiped in
  ignorance.

- They could return to worshiping the gods of Egypt from whom they had been delivered.
- They could worship the gods of the Canaanites whose land they had just conquered.

It seems almost unbelievable that they would even consider one of these alternatives. But before their time in the Promised Land was finished, the Israelites would virtually return to worshiping all three—in reverse order!

Conclusion

The greatness of Joshua's life can be summarized in the awesomeness of his ability as a soldier and as a leader. Years of being an understudy to Moses in the desert prepared Joshua to lead Israel in the conquest of the Promised Land. The tortured reminder of his past days in slavery enabled him to drive his soldiers on to total victory. He sought greatness for his country, not for himself.

True greatness is not in what we amass to ourselves, but in the service that we render to others. Joshua was a great man and a great leader because he had learned to be a good follower. He was a champion because he was committed to principles and to people.

God is looking for champions today like Joshua—men and women who will run ahead of the crowd and become leaders. Such leaders will not be embarrassed if they stumble and fall once in a while. They will not let their image or standing in society hold them back. If we are going to run our race for God and make a mark on our generation, we must tackle the opposition. Like Joshua, we must courageously step out for God—regardless of the circumstances.

FOUR
DAVID, THE SHEPHERD

NAME: David, meaning uncertain,
  perhaps "chieftain"
DATES: 1041—971 B.C.; ruled from
  1011—971 B.C.
CHARACTER QUALITY: Sincerity
SIGNIFICANCE: Ruled for 40 years as Israel's
  greatest king; author of many of the psalms
KEY TEXT: 1 Samuel 16:1, 10-13

DAVID'S life saw many phases: shepherd, singer, soldier, sinner, sovereign, and sage. He was both the sweet psalmist of Israel and the heroic slayer of Goliath. His was a life of balance. He knew when to pray and when to fight. The spiritual man never gives up. He does not faint. While others falter, lick their wounds, and wallow in self-pity, the spiritual man keeps on trusting God.

The Shepherd
The story of David is one of the most exciting adventures in all of the Bible. Here is a young man called of God out of total obscurity who rises to lead the nation of Israel and become its greatest king. He was selected by God Himself and anointed by the Prophet Samuel to replace Saul, who had failed as Israel's first king (1 Sam. 15:26).

When Samuel went to the house of Jesse in Bethlehem to anoint one of his eight sons to be the king of Israel, he was instructed by God, "Look not on his countenance, or on the height of his stature . . . for the Lord seeth not as man seeth; for man looketh on the outward appearance, but the Lord looketh on the heart" (16:7).

After Samuel had considered seven of Jesse's sons, he asked, " 'Are here all thy children?' And [Jesse] said, 'There remaineth yet the youngest, and behold, he keepeth the sheep.' And Samuel said unto Jesse, 'Send and fetch him.' . . .[David] was ruddy, and withal of a beautiful countenance, and goodly to look to. And the Lord said, 'Arise, anoint him; for this is he' " (16:11-12).

This anointing was done in private and was not intended to be a public announcement that David was king, but rather a prophetic and symbolic indication that David would *become* king officially at a later time. The Bible indicates that, from God's perspective, David was already His king (vv. 13-14)— even though he was only 16 years old and Saul still ruled Israel.

David had all of the ability and talent to rule as king, yet he had to wait for the sovereign timing of God before he could take the throne. Impressed by this experience with the Prophet Samuel, David had the patience to wait for the Lord's direction rather than put his hand against the Lord's anointed, Saul (24:6).

The Soldier

David's story shifts quickly from his obscure days as a shepherd to his opportunity to serve as both a singer and a soldier for Saul. David, who was God's choice to be king, was serving as a musician trying to soothe the mentally-deranged Saul (16:23). Later when the Philistine army moved up the valley of Elah, determined to capture Saul and exterminate the Israelite leadership, it was David who saved the day by defeating Goliath.

This incident of David's victory occurred when he was about 17 years old. David was not a little boy with a toy slingshot trying to attack a 30-foot tall fairy-tale giant. Rather, he was the age of a high school senior confronting a man who was over 9 feet tall and probably weighed close to 500 pounds.

For 40 days, morning and evening, Goliath had been harrassing the army of Israel.

> And [Goliath] stood and cried unto the armies of Israel. . . . "Choose you a man for you, and let him come down to me. If he be able to fight with me, and to kill me, then we will be your servants; but if I prevail against him, and kill him, then shall ye be our servants, and serve us.". . . When Saul and all Israel heard those words of the Philistine, they were dismayed, and greatly afraid (17:8-9, 11).

On the 41st morning, David responded to Goliath as if his challenge had been given for the very first time. In fact, David was disappointed that the army of Israel had not responded with greater confidence in God.

David believed that the Lord was strong enough to defeat Goliath. David said, "The Lord that delivered me out of the paw of the lion, and out of the paw of the bear, He will deliver me out of the hand of this Philistine" (17:37). With his slingshot and five smooth stones, David neared the mocking giant. David called out, "This day will the Lord deliver thee into mine hand. . . . And all this assembly shall know that the Lord saveth not with the sword and spear; for the battle is the Lord's and He will give you into our hands" (vv. 46-47).

Throughout this incident, David appears as a spiritually and morally superior person to Saul. In fact, it was Saul's cowardice that allowed him to send David into battle representing the army of Israel in the first place. Saul was "head and shoulders" taller than anyone else in Israel (9:2). If *anyone* should have confronted Goliath, it should have been *him*! But Saul was living in rebellion against God and as a result God raised up an enemy bigger than Saul to reveal his own inadequacy.

David's stunning victory over Goliath (17:49-51) was used by God to publically introduce him to the nation of Israel. God was letting the people know that all was not lost. The tragedy is that instead of viewing David as an ally who could help him in his fight against Israel's enemies, Saul jealously turned against David.

The Sought

At this point, much of David's story deals with his rejection by Saul and his friendship with Jonathan, Saul's son. The breakdown in David's relationship with Saul was caused by Saul's insecurity. First, Saul attempted to kill David (1 Sam. 18:11). When that didn't work, Saul demoted David from general to captain (v. 13); then he attempted to get David killed by giving him ridiculous assignments against the Philistines (chaps. 18—27). On one occasion, Saul ordered David to kill 100 Philistines and David killed 200! (18:25-27) After that, Saul threw a javelin at David, intending to kill him, but he missed (19:10). Finally, David escaped into the Judean wilderness for his life.

These must have been years of great difficulty for the young man who had been promised the crown of Israel. Instead of reigning from the throne, David wandered as a fugitive in Moab, among the Philistines, and in the Dead Sea caves of the Judean wilderness. During this time, David twice spared Saul's life—once in a cave in the wilderness of Engedi and again in the valley of the wilderness of Ziph (24:4-7; 26:7-12). Refusing to put his hand against the Lord's anointed, David finally emerged victorious.

During a battle with the Philistines at Mount Gilboa, Saul was wounded. Rather than be killed by the Philistines, Saul "took a sword and fell upon it" (31:4). The tragedy of Saul's life is that the one man who could have helped him defeat the Philistines, and who indeed finally *did* defeat them, was David. Instead of viewing his young friend as an ally, the insecure and bitter Saul drove David off into the wilderness. It was during these years that God developed tremendous patience in David.

The Sovereign

After Saul's death, David was anointed by the men of Judah to be their king. He was now about 30 years old and ruled over the tribe of Judah for the next seven years at Hebron. In the meantime, Abner, Saul's general, attempted to make Saul's son, Ishbosheth, the king over the eleven other tribes. After an attempted negotiation, Abner was assassinated by Joab, David's general. Ishbosheth was then assassinated by some of his own men, and David took the throne of *all* of Israel. However much blood unfortunately had been shed to acquire that throne: 85 priests whom Saul had assassinated; Saul and Jonathan and many of their soldiers were killed in battle; the Amalekite was executed; Abner and Ishbosheth were assassinated.

At this time, David was anointed king over all Israel at Hebron. This marked his third anointing (once privately by Samuel and twice publicly in the capital city of Judah). David immediately captured Jerusalem from the Jebusites and made it his permanent capital. He built a royal palace there and acquired materials for the building of the temple. He permanently defeated the Philistines and brought the ark of the covenant to Jerusalem.

It is as king that we see David at his greatest. Here is a man of wisdom, benevolence, and military genius who ruled his people under the hand of God. He was truly their shepherd. It was during this time that David was the recipient of the davidic covenant (2 Sam. 7:8-17). This covenant guaranteed the succession of his kingdom, promised that his son would build the temple, and that his throne would be established forever. It is this promise that causes those of us who know Christ as our Saviour to understand the permanence of God's

promises to the nation of Israel. We do not believe that all of
God's promises to Israel were fulfilled in the establishment of
the New Testament church. Rather, we are convinced that at
the end of the church age the millenial kingdom of Israel
shall come to pass on this earth. During this church age, the
Jewish people are still God's people and have a rightful claim
to the Land of Israel.

David's reign of peace and prosperity foreshadows the time
of blessing that shall come during the millenial age when
Christ shall rule the world from David's throne in Jerusalem.

The Sorrowful

There were many disappointments in David's life despite his
greatness. The greatest failure was his adultery with Bathsheba and the subsequent murder of her husband, Uriah.

At first, David attempted to cover up his sin by recalling
Uriah home from battle so that it would appear that Bathsheba had become pregnant by her own husband. But Uriah was
a dedicated soldier. He told David, "The ark, and Israel, and
Judah, abide in tents; and my lord Joab, and the servants of
my lord, are encamped in the open fields; shall I then go into
mine house, to eat and to drink, and to lie with my wife? As
thou livest, and as thy soul liveth, I will not do this thing"
(2 Sam. 11:11).

When this attempt failed, David became desperate. He
sent a sealed letter to Joab to arrange for Uriah's death in
battle. Then when Uriah was dead, David "fetched [Bathshe-
ba] to his house, and she became his wife, and bore him a
son. But the thing that David had done displeased the Lord"
(v. 27).

During this tragic time, David was confronted by the
Prophet Nathan. The man of God told David the parable
about the rich man who had many sheep, yet stole a pet lamb
from a poor farmer (12:1-4). David responded, "As the Lord
liveth, the man that hath done this thing shall surely die; and

he shall restore the lamb fourfold, because he did this thing, and because he had no pity" (vv. 5-6). Nathan then boldly pointed at David and announced, "Thou art the man!"

Unlike Saul, who constantly tried to excuse his own sin, David fully acknowledged that he had sinned against God. With bitter tears, David confessed his sin and genuinely repented (2 Sam. 12:13; Ps. 51). Even though God forgave David, He still judged him for his sin.

Within a few days, Bathsheba's baby died. In time, David's heart was broken by tragedies involving his sons Amnon, Absalom, Adonijah, and his daughter Tamar. Thus, his own verdict (fourfold restitution) literally came true within his own lifetime.

Even within this awful experience of David's sin with Bathsheba, we find hope and encouragement. The God who saves us is also the God who sustains us. The one who forgives our sins in Christ is the one who continues to forgive us throughout our walk with Him. David was never rejected because of his sin; rather, he was allowed to continue serving God. Through David's humiliation, God brought a greater spiritual maturity into his life.

This incident in David's life also teaches us never to give up on those who have failed. Often we reject someone who has failed in his Christian life, yet we offer God's forgiveness and salvation to other sinners who have never surrendered to Christ at all. When an unbelieving sinner with a terrible lifestyle comes to Christ, our tendency is to make an immediate hero out of him. But when a believer fails, our tendency is to turn against him.

God's dealings with David run contrary to that attitude. After this incident, Nathan became a close personal friend and advisor to David. Nathan stood with Bathsheba in insisting that her son Solomon should succeed David after his death. The very prophet who confronted David with his sin later stood as his advocate throughout his reign.

As preachers of God, we need to cry out against sin with

the boldness that Nathan had. But we must also develop
compassion. When sinners repent, we must be the first to
offer them the love of Christ as well.

The Statesman

After surviving Absalom's unsuccessful revolt, David emerged
as a grand statesman for the people of Israel. He expanded her
borders, reaffirmed her alliances, and prepared materials for
the construction of the temple, even handing the blueprints
over to Solomon (1 Chron. 22:6-16). David eventually raised
funds equivalent to $200 million in order to pay for the
temple by donating nearly half the amount himself. The
dedicatory offering included a thousand bulls, a thousand
rams, and a thousand lambs, all offered up as a burnt offering
unto the Lord.

At the height of his political power, David used his authority to point his people toward the Lord. His is an example
that every Christian leader should follow. David never forgot
who he was when God found him as a shepherd boy in the
hills near Bethlehem. In the palace in Jerusalem, David still
acknowledged that God had graciously put him there. Our
political leaders can take a great lesson from this. While ours
is not a theocracy as was ancient Israel, nevertheless those in
positions of political authority need to remember God as
David did.

The Scribe

In 2 Samuel 23:2 we read of David, "The Spirit of the Lord
was with me and in my tongue." As a result of divine
inspiration, David wrote over half the psalms and prophesied
of the coming of the Messiah more than any Old Testament
prophet. He predicted Christ's coming (Ps. 45:15), His rejection by Israel (Ps. 22:7); His betrayal (Ps. 41:9); His death
(Ps. 22:1-8); His burial (Ps. 49:15); His resurrection (Ps.

16:70); and His ascension (Ps. 16:18). David even talked about the future millennial kingdom on earth.

It is generally calculated that David wrote 77 of the 150 total psalms. Here we see the heart of the dear man of God; the expression of a man of God struggling with the crisis of life itself who was convinced that God is alive and He will bless those who put their faith and trust in Him. It is from his psalms that we really see David's heart. He raises us in the psalms to heights of ecstasy in the worship and praise of God Almighty. He drags us into the depths of despair and human agony, always noting that the Lord is my Shepherd!

Conclusion

No man but David has ever been called a man after God's own heart (Acts 13:22). David is a model for leadership in every generation. He knew the exhilaration of success and the agony of defeat. He was determined even to make his reversals count for God. He knew that he was nothing in himself, and thus we see the glory of God radiant in his life.

David's greatest quality was his sincerity. His shepherd's heart caused him to care for people with tender compassion. David was also a man of prayer. He knew how to communicate with God. Prayer is the most important, the most powerful force available to human beings.

Over my years in the pastorate, I have really learned to pray. When all the pressures of leadership come crashing down upon me, I know there is One who is greater than all my problems. When I turn to God and give my problems to Him, I find His place in the time of storm.

Finally, David was a man of perseverance. He never gave up when trouble came. If God's people will see nothing but the goal line, will accept nothing but victory, will pay any price, will suffer any hardship, will refuse to become discouraged, we cannot help but win. Filled with the Spirit of God, we can conquer any obstacle.

Despite his personal failures and successes, David was a man of integrity and sincerity. When challenged by the enemy, he volunteered for service. When confronted about his sin, he repented thoroughly. Through weakness and triumph, he remained a man of God.

In order to live successfully, you must forget those failures which are behind you. Many of us must learn to forget so that we can learn how to live. The person who succeeds is the one who will not accept defeat.

For David, it all began when he walked down into the valley alone to meet Goliath.

FIVE
ELIJAH, THE PROPHET

NAME: Elijah, "Jehovah is God"
DATES: 9th century B.C.
CHARACTER QUALITY: Boldness
SIGNIFICANCE: Greatest of the preaching
    prophets; went to heaven without dying
KEY TEXT: 1 Kings 17:1; 18:1, 20-24, 36-41

ELIJAH was the most fiery prophet of the Old Testament. Characterized by holy boldness, he was not afraid to confront kings, armies, enemies, false prophets, or anyone who opposed God. During his years of ministry, Elijah preached against the sins of Israel, killed the prophets of Baal, denounced the wickedness of Ahab and Jezebel, and struck soldiers with the fire of God.

Elijah was a crusader for righteousness. When the cause of God was at stake, he was there to defend it. He emerged on the scene when Israel was living in spiritual blindness and moral darkness. Unafraid of the opposition, Elijah set his face against the trend of the time and fought evil wherever he saw it. He is a model of courage and boldness to every preacher of God.

Prediction to King Ahab

Elijah's story is one of power. Here is one of the greatest prophets of God in confrontation with one of the most wicked kings of all time. Through Elijah's life, we see that God always raises up the right man at the right time to accomplish His purpose.

We know very little of Elijah's background. He was from the region of Gilead, east of the Jordan River. Scripture records nothing of his family background. He suddenly appeared upon the scene around 870 b.c. His ministry covered some 20 years of exciting and violent confrontation with the leaders of the Northern Kingdom of Israel.

Ahab was a cruel and ungodly king who had married Jezebel, a Phoenician princess. She was a fanatic devotee of the god Baal, commonly worshiped by the Phoenicians and the Canaanites as the storm god. Baal was generally depicted holding a lightning bolt in his hand. Hence, Elijah's confrontation with the prophets of Baal regarding the god who would answer by fire was most appropriate.

Elijah is one of those solitary individuals who appears from time to time in Scripture. Like John the Baptist in the New Testament, Elijah spent most of his life in isolation from people. Having made his astounding prediction to King Ahab, Elijah fled into the wilderness where he was miraculously fed by ravens. When the brook eventually dried up (1 Kings 17:7) because of the lack of rain which Elijah had predicted (v. 1), he was commanded of God to move to the north to Zidon, which was in Phoenicia.

Provision for a Widow

Elijah came to the village of Zarephath, a suburb of Zidon and stayed in a guest chamber owned by a poverty stricken widow and her son. When he arrived, he discovered that the widow was at the point of starvation. She told Elijah, "As the Lord thy God liveth, I have not a cake but an handful of meal in a barrel, and a little oil in a cruse; and, behold, I am gathering two sticks, that I may go in and dress it for me and my son, that we may eat it, and die" (1 Kings 17:12).

Elijah answered, "Make me thereof a little cake first, and bring it unto me, and after make for thee and for thy son. For thus saith the Lord God of Israel, 'The barrel of meal shall not waste, neither shall the cruse of oil fail, until the day that the Lord sendeth rain upon the earth' " (v. 14). The prophet remained there for many days and miraculously there was always a supply of meal and oil to meet their needs.

In time, the woman's son fell sick and died. Elijah carried the child up to the loft to his own bed and prayed over him three times until the soul of the child revived within him. This miraculous resurrection convinced the woman that Elijah was truly a man of God and that the Word of the Lord was in his mouth (vv. 17-21).

It is interesting to note that this woman lived in the very area from which Jezebel had come. Here was a pagan Phoenician woman caring for the prophet of Israel whose son was raised to life by the Lord. The incident indicates that what Ahab and Jezebel could not do in blessing the people of Israel, the Lord God could do for anyone who would trust in Him. It is also interesting that Jesus Himself referred to this event in His sermon at Nazareth. He remarked that there were many widows in the days of Elijah, but the prophet had only been sent to this one in the city of Sidon (Luke 4:25-26).

Proposal to the Prophets of Baal

After nearly three years, the Lord commanded Elijah to return to Ahab and announce the fulfillment of his prophecy. By this time, there was a terrible famine throughout the entire land. Even Ahab's capital city of Samaria was severely stricken.

Upon his return to Ahab, Elijah was asked by Ahab, "Art thou he that troubleth Israel?" (1 Kings 18:17) Elijah answered, "I have not troubled Israel; but thou, and thy father's house, in that ye have forsaken the commandments of the Lord, and thou hast followed Baalim" (v. 18). Elijah then challenged Ahab to a confrontation between himself and the

prophets of Baal upon Mount Carmel. This is a high mountain in northern Israel along the Mediterranean coast, which
overlooks modern-day Haifa on one side and the Valley of
Jezreel on the other side. It was here that the 450 prophets of
Baal came to confront Elijah (vv. 19-20).

Elijah spoke to the crowd which had gathered and asked
them, "How long halt thee between two opinions? If the Lord
be God, follow Him; but if Baal, then follow him" (v. 21).
The people were so stunned at his boldness that they did not
answer a word. Therefore, Elijah proposed a contest to deter-
mine which god was indeed the true God.

> Then said Elijah unto the people, "I, even I only,
> remain a prophet of the Lord; but Baal's prophets
> are 450 men. Let them therefore give us two bull-
> ocks; and let them choose one bullock for them-
> selves, and cut it in pieces, and lay it on wood, and
> put no fire under, and I will dress the other bull-
> ock, and lay it on wood, and put no fire under; and
> call ye on the name of your gods, and I will call on
> the name of the Lord; and the God that answereth
> by fire, let him be God." And all the people
> answered and said, "It is well spoken" (18:22-24).

Elijah allowed the prophets of Baal to select their own
bullock and to attempt to get Baal to answer by fire. It should
be noted here that Elijah was challenging Baal at the very
source of his supposed strength. Elijah was demanding that
the god of the lightning bolts answer by fire.

Throughout the entire morning of the contest, the prophets of Baal worked themselves into a frenzy. They "called on
the name of Baal from morning even until noon, saying, 'O
Baal, hear us.' But there was no voice, nor any that answered.
And they leaped upon the altar which was made. . . . And
they cried aloud, and cut themselves after their manner with
knives and lancets, till the blood gushed out upon them" (vv.
26, 28).

By noon Elijah began to mock them, saying, "Cry aloud;

for [Baal] is a god; either he is talking, or he is pursuing, or he is in a journey, or peradventure he sleepeth, and must be awaked" (v. 27). Finally during the afternoon Elijah called the people to come together and repair the altar of the Lord which had been broken down (v. 30).

Principles of revival in this passage are many. In order to turn the nation around, Elijah was convinced that the altar of the Lord had to be repaired and the sacrifice had to be put in order properly. To convince the people that it was the Lord Jehovah who alone could answer by fire, Elijah demanded that the sacrifice be soaked three times with four barrels of water each time. The altar became so drenched that the water filled a trench which ran around the altar (vv. 31-35).

Since it had not rained by this time for three and a half years, it is possible that Elijah's request for the precious water was granted because of the unique nature of the confronta-tion, or that it was salt water obtained from the Mediterra-nean Sea below. The text never makes it clear as to the source of the water.

When the sacrifice was ready, Elijah prayed:

> Lord God of Abraham, Isaac, and of Israel, let it be known this day that Thou art God in Israel, and that I am Thy servant, and that I have done all these things at Thy word. Hear me, O Lord, hear me, that this people may know that Thou art the Lord God, and that Thou hast turned their heart back again (vv. 36-37).

Elijah's prayer was brief and powerful. As a result, "The fire of the Lord fell, and consumed the burnt sacrifice, and the wood, and the stones, and the dust, and licked up the water that was in the trench. And when all the people saw it, they fell on their faces; and they said, 'The Lord, He is the God; the Lord, He is the God' " (vv. 38-39).

In the frenzy that resulted, Elijah took the prophets of Baal and killed them all. He then announced that it was going to rain immediately (v. 41). When Elijah sent his servant to the top of Mount Carmel to look out over the Mediterranean Sea, the servant came back and reported that there was nothing there but a cloudless sky.

Finally on the servant's seventh attempt, he returned and said that there was a little cloud arising above the sea "like a man's hand" (v. 44). Elijah, convinced that the storm was on its way, then instructed everyone to get down from the mountain because of the danger of flash flooding. The heavens immediately became black with clouds; there was a violent wind and rain storm as Ahab rode his chariot down the mountain toward the Valley of Jezreel. In the meantime, the hand of the Lord "was on Elijah, and he girded up his loins, and ran before Ahab to the entrance of Jezreel" (v. 46).

It is so easy in a time of spiritual drought to give up on the reality of the power of God. I have many times called this nation to revival and gone and looked at the distant spiritual horizon to see nothing more than a little cloud, about the size of a man's hand. I am convinced that we are living in a time when God is preparing to do great things. While others may decry the absence of showers of refreshing, I am convinced that we will never see revival until:

We repair the altar of the Lord, and

We confront the false prophets of our day.

Until we are spiritually prepared to be all that God wants us to be, and until we are willing to cry out against false religion, humanism, and secularism, we will never have revival.

Plight in the Wilderness

One would think that Elijah would now be at the height of his preaching career. However, when he learned that Jezebel was so angered by what had happened at Mount Carmel that she wanted to kill him, he fled into the wilderness. Emotionally and physically exhausted, Elijah fell down and begged God to let him die. "O Lord, take away my life; for I am not better than my fathers" (1 Kings 19:4).

So desperate was Elijah's fear that when he reached Beersheba, in the south, he traveled forty days beyond that into the Sinai wilderness! "And [Elijah] arose, and did eat and drink, and went in the strength of that meat forty days and forty nights unto Horeb the mount of God. And he came thither unto a cave, and lodged there"(vv. 8-9).

It was in Elijah's moment of greatest need that the Lord began to call to him in the cave, "What doest thou here, Elijah?" (v. 9) Elijah responded, "I have been very jealous for the Lord God of hosts; for the Children of Israel have forsaken Thy covenant, thrown down Thine altars, and slain Thy prophets with the sword; and I, even I only, am left; and they seek my life, to take it away" (v. 10).

God told Elijah to go out of the cave and stand on the mountain. "And, behold, the Lord passed by, and a great and strong wind rent the mountains, and brake in pieces the rocks before the Lord; but the Lord was not in the wind; and after the wind an earthquake; but the Lord was not in the earthquake; and after the earthquake a fire; but the Lord was not in the fire" (vv. 11-12).

After the fire Elijah could hear a still, small voice calling to him. "What doest thou here, Elijah? . . . Go, return on thy way to the wilderness of Damascus" (vv. 13, 15).

There in the very place where God appeared to Moses and spoke to him, He rebuked Elijah and ordered him to return to public service. Elijah's life was certainly not over, for God intended for him to do three tasks that would change the course of history. He was to go to Damascus, the capital of Syria, the enemy of Israel and anoint Hazael to be Syria's next king. Elijah was then to anoint Jehu to be the next king over Israel. Finally, Elijah was to anoint Elisha to be the prophet who would eventually replace him (vv. 15-16).

In obedience to God's command, Elijah left the cave, returned to Israel, and found Elisha plowing in a field with twelve yoke of oxen before him.

And Elijah passed by [Elisha], and cast his mantle upon him. And he left the oxen, and ran after Elijah, and said, "Let me, I pray thee, kiss my father and my mother, and then I will follow thee."

And he said unto him, "Go back again; for what have I done to thee?"

And [Elisha] returned back from [Elijah] . . . and gave unto the people, and they did eat. Then [Elisha] arose, and went after Elijah, and ministered unto him (vv. 19-21).

Pronouncement of Ahab's Doom

In the meantime, Ahab became jealous of the vineyard of Naboth, which was near his palace. When the king offered to buy the vineyard or trade property to acquire it, Naboth realized that such was forbidden in the Law of Moses. The Law demanded that property remain within given families since that property was considered the "inheritance of the Lord" (Lev. 25:23). Ahab intended to violate the Law, but Naboth refused to cooperate with his sin.

The enraged Jezebel then plotted to have Naboth stoned to death.

[Jezebel] wrote letters in Ahab's name . . . and sent the letters unto the elders and to the nobles that were in [Naboth's] city. And she wrote in the letters . . . "Set two men, sons of Belial, before [Naboth], to bear witness against him, saying, 'Thou didst blaspheme God and the king.' And then carry him out and stone him, that he may die." And the men of his city . . . did as Jezebel had sent unto them. . . . Then they carried [Naboth] forth out of the city, and stoned him. . . . Then they sent to Jezebel saying, "Naboth is stoned and is dead" (1 Kings 21:8-11, 13-14).

Afterward, when Ahab went to take possession of Naboth's property, Elijah met him in the vineyard. Stunned by the sudden reappearance of the mighty prophet, Ahab asked, "Hast thou found me, O mine enemy?" (v. 20) Elijah's answer was severe: "In the place where dogs licked the blood of Naboth shall dogs lick thy blood. . . . The dogs shall eat Jezebel by the wall of Jezreel" (vv. 19, 23).

Three years later, Ahab was killed in a battle against Syria. While his body was taken for burial and a servant washed his bloodied armor, the dogs licked his blood out of the bottom of the chariot (22:38). Several years later, after Elijah had gone to heaven, Jezebel was assassinated by Jehu. Having driven his chariot to her palace at Jezreel, Jehu demanded that Jezebel's eunuchs throw her off a balcony. When they did so, Jehu trampled her with his chariot and left her bloody body splattered on the ground. In the meantime, the wild dogs came and ate her remains (2 Kings 9:30-37).

Preparation of Elisha

Elijah was such a fiery prophet of God that he never really reached his peak until he departed for heaven. After Ahab's death, Ahab's son Ahaziah fell through the lattice of his upper chamber in the palace of Samaria. While upon his deathbed, he sent his servants to inquire of the prophets of Baal as to whether he would recover. Instead, Elijah met them and rebuked them for their continued idolatry. When the king asked his servants what kind of man had spoken to them, they answered, "He was a hairy man, and girt with a girdle of leather about his loins" (2 Kings 1:8). The king responded, "It is Elijah!"

When Ahaziah sent a captain of 50 soldiers to arrest Elijah, the prophet struck them dead with fire from heaven. The second attempt ended the same way. Finally, the third captain came, fell down before Elijah, and begged him for his life. The prophet went with the soldier to meet the king. He told Ahaziah that he would die; then Elijah left.

Before he died, Elijah established a school of prophets, of which Elisha was the star pupil. On the last day of Elijah's life, he was so busy that Elisha could hardly keep up with him. The Lord sent Elijah from Gilgal to Bethel, to Jericho, and finally down to the Jordan River (2 Kings 2:1-6). Each time he moved on, Elijah asked Elisha if he wanted to remain behind, but Elisha insisted on going with him. When they finally reached the Jordan, Elijah "took his mantle, and wrapped it together, and smote the waters, and they were divided hither and thither, so that they two went over on dry ground" (v. 8).

> And Elisha said, "I pray thee, let a double portion of thy spirit be upon me."
>
> And [Elijah] said, "Thou hast asked a hard thing; nevertheless, if thou see me when I am taken from thee, it shall be so unto thee; but if not, it shall not be so."
>
> And it came to pass, as they still went on, and talked, that, behold, there appeared a chariot of fire, and horses of fire, and parted them both asunder; and Elijah went up by a whirlwind into heaven (vv. 9-11).

How appropriate! The fiery, old prophet departed even as he had lived. However, he did not go on to heaven without leaving behind proper preparation for the ongoing of his prophetic ministry. Elijah left behind trained preachers (sons of the prophets) to continue spreading the Word of the Lord to the nation of Israel. He also left behind his mantle, which Elisha used to part the waters of the Jordan as he returned to the west bank (v. 14).

Conclusion

A true champion of God does not merely make an outstand ing contribution himself, but he sees the need to train others to serve the Lord as well. When Elijah thought he was standing all alone, he collapsed in depression and despair. But when he realized that there were 7,000 in Israel who had not bowed to Baal (1 Kings 19:18) and that there was still hope for revival, he committed himself to the training of young men who would multiply his ministry.

As the chancellor of Liberty Baptist College, I have been burdened to transfer the biblical concepts which have molded my life to the lives of young people who could multiply my ministry far beyond that which I could ever do alone. If there was ever a man in Scripture who appeared to be a lone wolf, it was certainly Elijah. Yet the greatest contribution that he made was in the training of young men to take his place when he was gone.

Elijah was also a man of prayer. He prayed that it would not rain for three years. The ensuing drought was a slap in the face of Baal, the Canaanite storm god, who supposedly controlled the weather. Elijah also prayed that God would consume his sacrifice with fire from heaven. Then he prayed that it would rain and end the drought. In all these cases, Elijah was victorious by the overcoming power of prayer.

Like Elijah, we need to learn that nothing of real significance in this world is ever accomplished apart from prayer.

SIX
ELISHA,
THE MIRACLE-WORKER

NAME: Elisha, "God is salvation"
DATES: 9th century B.C.; about 870—790 B.C.
CHARACTER QUALITY: Devotion
SIGNIFICANCE: Understudy to Elijah;
    succeeded him as the head of the
    "School of the Prophets"
KEY TEXT: 1 Kings 19:19-21; 2 Kings 2:9-15

ELIJAH and Elisha represent a total contrast in personalities, yet both were called men of God. "Let thy mantle fall on me" was the cry of Elisha's life. He begged for a double portion of Elijah's spirit. Indeed, he was in many ways more successful than his predecessor Elijah, to whom he was sincerely devoted.

Elisha was quieter and less outlandish than Elijah. Elisha never called down fire from heaven, but he performed more recorded miracles than Elijah. He also organized and perpetrated the "School of the Prophets" to train young men to preach the Word of God.

Preparation by Elijah

Elisha came to the most important decision of his life in a most unexpected way. He was plowing at the end of the line, eating the dust of all the others before him, when the mighty prophet found him. Elijah ran past him and cast his mantle upon him and kept going. However, Elisha ran after him and said, "Let me, I pray thee, kiss my father and my mother, and then I will follow thee" (1 Kings 19:20).

Elijah was shocked by Elisha's response and rebuked him. Instead of returning to his parents, Elisha returned and took the yoke of oxen and killed them and burned the plow. He was literally burning his bridges behind him!

For the next several years, Elisha was an understudy to Elijah. Scripture refers to the "sons of the prophets," that is, a school of prophets who studied under Elijah. Elisha was evidently the valedictorian of the class! When the time came for Elijah to be taken to heaven, he busily moved from town to town on his last day on earth and continued to ask Elisha if he wanted to remain behind. However, Elisha responded that he would not leave him until Elijah was taken up. Then Elisha made his request that a "double portion" of Elijah's spirit rest upon him (2 Kings 2:9). The request was in essence a plea for empowerment. Elijah's response was that if you see me when I go up, you will have it.

Suddenly, the chariot of fire appeared and parted the two of them. Elisha cried, "My father, my father, the chariot of Israel, and the horseman thereof " (v. 12). As Elijah went up to heaven in a whirlwind, his mantle fell behind at Elisha's feet. The great moment of truth had come. Taking up the mantle, Elisha returned to the Jordan River with one question in his mind: Could he part the Jordan River as Elijah had done?

Scripture tells us that the sons of the prophets stood on the opposite bank of the Jordan River at Jericho, watching to see whether the spirit of Elijah did indeed rest upon Elisha. The younger prophet took the mantle and threw it into the waters asking, "Where is the Lord God of Elijah?" (v. 14) Immediately, the waters parted and Elisha walked over on dry ground. He was recognized by the school of the prophets as a "prophet of God indeed" and their leader.

Most of the recorded history of Elisha's life revolves around his many unusual miracles. Elisha was empowered by God to do things that no one else had ever done. Some of his miracles were not spectacular, such as causing an axhead to swim; but each was a genuine miracle of God. These miracles attracted the attention of Israel to the message that Elisha preached.

Purifying the Waters of Jericho

Upon crossing the Jordan River, one of Elisha's first miracles was that of purifying a polluted well at Jericho by pouring a bowl of salt into the noxious water.

> And Elisha went forth unto the spring of waters, and cast the salt in there, and said, "Thus saith the Lord, 'I have healed these waters; there shall not be from thence any more death or barren land.'" So the waters were healed unto this day, according to the saying of Elisha (2 Kings 2:21-22).

This was similar to the miracle done by Moses at Marah centuries before (Ex. 15:23-25).

Providing Water in the Desert

Jehoshaphat, king of Judah, and Jehoram, king of Israel, had formed an alliance with the king of Edom to battle the Moabites. As the three kings and their armies crossed the desert of Edom, there was no water to be found. The three kings consulted with Elisha for direction from the Lord. Elisha instructed:

> Make this valley full of ditches. For thus saith the Lord, "Ye shall not see wind, neither shall ye see rain; yet that valley shall be filled with water, that ye may drink, both ye, and your cattle, and your beasts" (2 Kings 3:16-17).

This miracle actually led to the defeat of the Moabites. For the Moabites "rose up early in the morning, and the sun shone upon the water, and the Moabites saw the water on the other side as red as blood; and they said, 'This is blood; the kings are surely slain, and they have smitten one another;

now therefore, Moab, to the spoil' " (vv. 22-23). But when
the Moabites reached the camp of Israel, they were badly
defeated (vv. 24-25).

Providing Oil in Empty Vessels

At Samaria, the capital of the Northern Kingdom, Elisha
rescued a poverty-stricken widow from her creditors.

> Then [Elisha] said, "Go, borrow thee vessels
> abroad of all thy neighbors, even empty vessels;
> borrow not a few. And when thou art come in,
> thou shalt shut the door upon thee and upon thy
> sons, and shalt pour out [thy oil supply] into all
> those vessels, and thou shalt set aside that which is
> full."
>
> So she went out from him, and. . . poured out.
> And it came to pass, when the vessels were full,
> that she. . . . came and told the man of God.
>
> And he said, "Go, sell the oil, and pay thy debt,
> and live thou and thy children of the rest" (2 Kings
> 4:3-7).

These first three miracles performed by the Prophet Elisha
were indications of God's miraculous provision for His
children.

Raising the Dead Boy at Shunem

In Shunem Elisha was provided with a room to sleep in by a
prominent woman and her husband. To reward her kindness,
Elisha prophesied that the woman would have a son.
" 'About this season, according to the time of life, thou shalt
embrace a son.' . . . And the woman conceived, and bare a
son at that season that Elisha had said unto her" (2 Kings
4:16-17).

However, after the son was born, he fell sick some years
later and died. In response to her pleading, Elisha returned to
Shunem with the woman.

And when Elisha was come into the house, behold, the child was dead, and laid upon his bed. . . . And [Elisha] went up, and lay upon the child, and put his mouth upon his mouth, and his eyes upon his eyes, and his hands upon his hands; and he stretched himself upon the child; and the flesh of the child waxed warm. . . . And the child opened his eyes (4:32, 34-35).

Healing Naaman the Syrian

One of Elisha's most unusual miracles was that of healing Naaman, the commander of the Syrian army. Naaman, who was a leper, had an Israeli slave girl who worked in his household. This young girl told Naaman of the miraculous power of the Prophet Elisha. So Naaman sought after Elisha, hoping to be healed.

When he arrived at Elisha's house, Naaman was met by Elisha's servant who instructed him, "Go and wash in Jordan seven times, and thy flesh shall come again to thee, and thou shalt be clean" (2 Kings 5:10).

Naaman was very upset that Elisha would not even meet with him, but instead had sent a servant to relay the instructions from the Lord. Naaman had expected that Elisha would call on the Lord's name and immediately heal him.

Though Naaman was angry, he was finally persuaded by his servant to obey the command. "Then went [Naaman] down, and dipped himself seven times in Jordan, according to the saying of the man of God; and his flesh came again like unto the flesh of a little child, and he was clean" (v. 14).

When Naaman returned to Elisha's home with gifts for the prophet, he was met by Elisha himself who refused the gifts. Tragically, Elisha's servant Gehazi secretly pursued Naaman and begged the rewards for himself. When Gehazi returned to Elisha, he tried to hide what he had done from the prophet. But Elisha confronted him with these words:

Went not mine heart with thee, when the man
turned again from his chariot to meet thee? Is it a
time to receive money, and to receive garments,
and olive yards, and vineyards, and sheep, and
oxen, and menservants, and maidservants? The
leprosy therefore of Naaman shall cleave unto
thee, and unto thy seed forever (5:26-27).

This entire incident reveals the merciful heart of God even
to the enemies of Israel and the severity of God's judgment
even upon the people of Israel.

Recovering a Lost Axhead

At the Jordan River, the sons of the prophets were building a
house. "As one was felling a beam, the axhead fell into the
water; and he cried, and said, 'Alas, master! For it was
borrowed.' And [Elisha] said, 'Where fell it?' And he showed
him the place. And [Elisha] cut down a stick, and cast it in
thither; and the iron did swim" (2 Kings 6:5-6).

The contrast of these miracles—from raising a dead boy
back to life, to causing an axhead to swim—shows us God is
interested in *all* of our problems, both big and small.

Blinding the Syrian Army

Elisha warned the King of Israel of several planned Syrian
ambushes (2 Kings 6:8-10). When the Syrian king found out
about this, he attempted to arrest Elisha. "Therefore sent he
thither horses, and chariots, and a great host; and they came
by night, and compassed the city about" (v. 14).

When Elisha's servant woke up and saw that the city was
surrounded, he told Elisha. But the prophet wasn't worried.
He said, "Fear not; for they that be with us are more than
they that be with them" (v. 16). The servant's eyes were
opened by the Lord and "behold, the mountain was full of
horses and chariots of fire round about Elisha. And when they

came down to him, Elisha prayed unto the Lord. . . . And
[the Lord] smote [the Syrians] with blindness according to the
word of Elisha" (vv. 17-18).

The prophet then led the blinded army into Israelite Samaria. This miracle was done to prove that God was greater
than Israel's enemies.

Predicting Israel's Victory Over Syria

Some years later, the Syrians invaded Israel again and be-
sieged the capital city of Samaria, causing a great famine. The
famine was so severe that some people even resorted to
cannibalism in order to survive (2 Kings 6:29). The Israelite
king tried to blame the entire incident on Elisha (v. 31).

Elisha ignored the king's threats and predicted that in 24
hours, food would be so plentiful that the people would be
virtually giving it away! "Tomorrow about this time shall a
measure of fine flour be sold for a shekel, and two measures of
barley for a shekel, in the gate of Samaria" (7:1).

Outside the gate of the city, four starving lepers decided in
desperation to surrender to the Syrians and began walking
toward their camp during the night.

> And they rose up in the twilight to go unto the
> camp of the Syrians; and when they were come to
> the . . . camp of Syria, behold, there was no man
> there. For the Lord had made the host of the
> Syrians to hear a noise of chariots, and a noise of
> horses, even the noise of a great host. . . . Where-
> fore [the Syrians] arose and fled (7:5-7).

Finally on his deathbed, Elisha predicted Israel's three
consecutive victories over Syria (13:14-19).

Posthumous Miracle

One of the strangest miracles in all of the Bible was recorded
after Elisha's death. A short time afterward, during a Moabite

invasion, some men were burying a man, when they spotted the invading horde. Quickly, they threw the body into Elisha's sepulcher. When the dead man's body touched the bones of Elisha, the dead man "revived, and stood on his feet" (2 Kings 13:21). Thus, even though Elisha was dead, he is credited with performing the only posthumous miracle in the Bible!

Conclusion

Elisha was one of the most unusual prophets who ever lived. However, he was called by God out of a very common background. Elisha was an ordinary man whose life had been touched by God's extraordinary power. Like other great champions, he learned to become a good leader by first being a good follower.

In Elisha's ministry, we see that he had a heart for the poor. I believe that American Christians need broken hearts for the poor and hurting around the world. Not only do we need to win them to Christ, but we also need to meet their practical needs. We should be concerned that they have adequate medical treatment. We need to be earnestly involved in helping the poor and needy so that the message of the Gospel will be received by them. We cannot merely give them a "God bless you." We must be willing to show them that Jesus does indeed care about their burdens and problems.

Another important principle we see in Elisha's life is that of reaching beyond our own national boundaries. Elisha took mercy on Naaman, the Syrian general. Our nationalism probably would have told most of us to turn our backs on a person like Naaman. But the prophet of God showed Naaman the reality of the living Lord by extending a hand of mercy. I am convinced that if we are to effectively fulfill the Great Commission we must reach out to the hurting people beyond our own shores.

We also see in Elisha's story the importance of the providence of God. Every time he faced danger, Elisha trusted in the Lord. God provided His guardian angels to watch over and protect Elisha. The prophet was able to see the invisible, rather than being limited by the visible. A true sense of spiritual vision allows us to see the world as God sees it.

From Elisha's posthumous miracle we learn that a work done for God is eternal in its consequence. The Scripture says of Abel, he "being dead yet speaketh" (Heb. 11:4). As we train others to serve the Lord, they become eternal monuments of God's grace. Investing in bricks and mortar is only a necessity in order to invest in flesh and blood. The goal in any Christian ministry ought not to be in how many buildings we can build, but in how many lives we can influence. Long after those buildings have crumbled, the living monuments of God's grace—like Elisha—will carry God's message to the next generation.

SEVEN
DANIEL, THE STATESMAN

NAME: Daniel, "God is my Judge"
DATES: 620—536 B.C.
CHARACTER QUALITY: Dependability
SIGNIFICANCE: Greatest predicting prophet;
     lived through the entire 70-year Babylonian
     Captivity, serving as a political advisor
     to Nebuchadnezzar, Belshazzar, and Darius.
KEY TEXT: Daniel 1:1-8

FROM his early teenage years Daniel displayed the qualities
of dependability and responsibility which made him great.
Those qualities produced Daniel's other characteristics of
wisdom, leadership, and commitment. When the pressure
was on, he never succumbed.

There are times when every leader must do what he be-
lieves is right, even if the cost of doing it is very great. In
1979 when I first announced my plans to launch the Moral
Majority and get involved in our nation's social and political
life, many of my closest associates tried to discourage me.
They argued that preachers had no place in politics. But then
I remembered Daniel. He was a devout servant of God. Yet
he was thoroughly involved in the political life of both the
Babylonian and Persian empires.

In his lifetime, Daniel faced many life-threatening situa-
tions, but he did not back down. His faith in God drove him
on to greatness in an hour when most of his countrymen were
lagging behind. Though he grew up in a foreign empire in an
atmosphere of compromise, he "purposed in his heart" not to
fail God. He was dependable right to the end.

Many of the events of Daniel's life may be compared to

those in the life of Joseph. Both were illegitimately thrown into jail and both had the gift of interpreting dreams. Both rose to power under the leading rulers of their day. Both were righteous men whose lives were given to the service of God. Like Joseph, the quality that most characterized Daniel's life was his determined purpose and conviction.

A Man of Purpose

The Chaldeans, a small elite ruling class, controlled the Babylonian empire during Nebuchadnezzar's reign. King Nebuchadnezzar himself was a member of that ruling class. To guard against losing his political power, Nebuchadnezzar gathered young captives from the ruling family of Judah to train as potential future statesmen for the Babylonian empire.

Daniel, being of royal descent (Dan. 1:3), was chosen to enter the three-year training program set up by King Nebuchadnezzar. The young people chosen for this special training were "well favored, and skillful in all wisdom, and cunning in knowledge, and understanding science" (v. 4). The goal of the training program was to teach these exceptional children the wisdom of the Chaldeans.

As trainees in the king's special course, Daniel and his three friends, Hananiah, Mishael, and Azariah, were taught the language of the Chaldeans and were given Babylonian names—Shadrach, Meshach, and Abednego. Daniel was renamed Belteshazzar. This was all done to break down their national identity and force them to comply with Babylonian ways.

The trainees were offered the best of the king's food and wine. However, Daniel and his friends refused to partake of the royal menu because it would violate their religious convictions. They determined that they would not go against the Lord.

We must remember that these were teenage boys who were a long way from home. They had been taken into captivity, and disobedience might have cost them their lives. Nevertheless, they stood firm in their convictions.

We are not told what was wrong with the king's food. It may have been blessed by false gods or it may have been in violation of Mosaic Law. As a creative alternative, Daniel made this suggestion to the eunuch in charge: "Prove thy servants, I beseech thee, ten days; and let them give us pulse to eat, and water to drink. Then let our countenance be looked upon before thee, and the countenance of the children that eat of the portion of the king's meat; and as thou seest, deal with thy servants" (vv. 12-13).

At the end of the ten-day period, Daniel and his friends were "fairer and fatter in flesh than all the children which did eat of the king's meat" (v. 15). By the end of the three-year program, Daniel and his three friends were ten times superior to all of the other trainees (v. 20).

Scripture makes it clear that we are to obey the laws of man (Rom. 13:1-3), unless those laws violate the laws of God. God is always looking for men and women who will stand up for righteousness no matter what the cost may be. It is so easy for us to offer every kind of excuse to compromise with sin. But God blesses conviction, not compromise. Daniel's stand of courage indicates his true greatness. He was not a great champion merely because he predicted the future, but because he stood firm in his convictions.

Man of Courage

As we read the Book of Daniel, a great deal of time passes quickly from chapter to chapter. Daniel was taken captive when he was about 15 years old and at 18 he completed the training program. While he was still in school, he interpreted an unusual dream of Nebuchadnezzar's.

Nebuchadnezzar had had a troubling dream, and even though the king couldn't remember his dream, he still wanted his wise men to explain it to him. Nebuchadnezzar said:

> The thing is gone from me; if ye will not make known unto me the dream, with the interpretation thereof, ye shall be cut in pieces. . . . But if ye show me the dream, and the interpretation thereof, ye shall receive of me gifts and rewards and great honor (Dan. 2:5-6).

The magicians, sorcerers, astrologers, and wise Chaldeans couldn't believe that Nebuchadnezzar would make such an outrageous demand. "There is not a man upon the earth that can show the king's matter," they told Nebuchadnezzar (v. 10).

The king became very angry and "commanded to destroy all the wise men of Babylon. And the decree went forth . . . and they sought Daniel and his fellows to be slain" (vv. 12-13). But Daniel courageously spoke up and promised to interpret Nebuchadnezzar's dream (v. 16).

Immediately, Daniel and his three Hebrew friends prayed together about this matter. "Then was the secret revealed unto Daniel in a night vision. Then Daniel blessed the God of heaven" (v. 19).

Daniel interpreted Nebuchadnezzar's dream of the gigantic metallic statue and explained its prophetic significance (vv. 27-45). The king was so grateful that he "made Daniel a great man, and gave him many great gifts, and made him ruler over the whole province of Babylon, and chief of the governors over all the wise men of Babylon" (v. 48).

After this incident, King Nebuchadnezzar built a huge statue of gold and commanded:

> At what time ye hear the sound of . . . all kinds of music, ye fall down and worship the golden image . . . and whoso falleth not down and worshippeth shall the same hour be cast into the midst of a burning fiery furnace (3:5-6).

When Daniel's three friends were commanded to bow down before the golden image, they told Nebuchadnezzar, "Our God whom we serve is able to deliver us from the burning fiery furnace. . . . But if not, be it known unto thee, O King, that we will not serve thy gods, nor worship the golden image" (vv. 17-18).

Nebuchadnezzar was "full of fury" and commanded that the three Hebrews be bound and thrown into the burning flames (vv. 19, 21). Later on when the king looked into the furnace to see whether the three Hebrews had been killed, he saw "four men loose . . . and they have no hurt; and the form of the fourth is like the Son of God" (v. 25). The courage of the three Hebrews made their deliverance all the more spectacular.

Daniel was also a man of great courage. He was willing to stand against the greatest kings of his day and pronounce God's judgment against them. When he interpreted the tree vision of Nebuchadnezzar, he told the king with a broken heart that he (the king) was the tree which would be cut down. Nebuchadnezzar's pride would cause his fall from the throne for seven years.

Daniel predicted, "They shall drive thee from men, and thy dwelling shall be with the beasts of the field, and they shall make thee to eat grass as oxen . . . till thou know that the Most High ruleth" (4:25). A year later, Nebuchadnezzar walked into his palace and said, "Is not this great Babylon, that I have built . . . by the might of my power, and for the honor of my majesty?" (v. 30) While he was still speaking, the judgment of God came upon him. The king was driven from men and lived like a wild animal for seven years. Then his understanding returned and he "blessed the Most High" (v. 34).

Throughout his life, Daniel's sense of purpose and conviction produced an abundance of courage. As an old man, Daniel stood before King Belshazzar and told him that his kingdom was finished. He predicted that the kingdom would be divided among the Medes and the Persians. That same night was "Belshazzar the king of the Chaldeans slain. And Darius the Median took the kingdom" (5:30-31).

A Man of Prayer

When the new administration came to power, Darius the Mede was made governor over Babylon under the Persian emperor Cyrus. Daniel, now in his mid 80s, was promoted to a place of significant leadership over the hierarchy of the rulers of the province (Dan. 6:2). But the other jealous leaders attempted to find a reason to accuse him to the king. However, Daniel was so faithful and dependable in his service to the king that they found nothing against him except "concerning the law of his God" (Dan. 6:5). The jealous leaders secretly went to Darius and suggested that he make a 30-day law against praying to any deity or person other than himself (vv. 7-9).

Unlike the autocratic Chaldean rulers, the kings of the Medes and Persians were unable to change their own laws (v. 15). When the law was announced, Daniel refused to comply. He knelt in his house with the windows open toward Jerusalem and prayed three times a day unto God (v. 10). He was arrested, convicted, and cast into the den of lions against Darius' objections (vv. 14, 16-18).

Early the next morning, Darius hurried to the lions' den to check on Daniel. Daniel called out to him, "My God hath sent His angel, and hath shut the lions' mouths" (v. 22). The king was very happy and had Daniel released. Then the men who had accused Daniel were thrown to the lions (v. 24).

Daniel's prayer life is not only recorded in this incident, but in many of his subsequent prophetic passages as well. It was during a season of lengthy prayer that God revealed to him the mystery of the 70 weeks which were determined upon the people of Israel (9:24-27). On another occasion he prayed and fasted three entire weeks during a time of crisis (10:2-3). Daniel was such a godly man that he even confessed the sins of the nation of Israel to the Lord (chap. 9). He begged for God's mercy and for His protection for the people of Israel. Daniel died in Babylon, but as a result of his prayer, God sent others to rebuild Jerusalem and the temple there.

We also read that Daniel was a man of the book. While he was reading from Jeremiah's writings, he realized that the 70-year captivity was nearly over (9:2). Recognizing that Israel had become complacent in the years of her captivity, Daniel pleaded with God to return them to the land where they might serve the Lord.

It is interesting to note that the Book of Daniel clearly tells us that Daniel read from the inspired prophecies of Jeremiah. The Book of Ezekiel refers to Daniel as one of the great men of the Old Testament era. If these men who were inspired of God to write His Word, were reading each other's prophecies, how much more do we today need to thoroughly study the Word of God!

A Man of Vision
Daniel predicted the rise and fall of four subsequent Gentile world powers: Babylon, Medea-Persia, Greece, and Rome (Dan. 2; 7). He also predicted the defeat of the Persians by Alexander the Great (chap. 8). He further predicted the coming of Christ and the coming of the antichrist (chap. 11). In the last chapter of his prophecy, he predicted the conditions which would prevail in the last days (chap. 12). Daniel's prophecies were apocalyptic in nature, as are the prophecies of the Book of Revelation. Daniel's prophecy of the 70 weeks (chap. 9) forms the basis of our understanding of an eschatological timetable related to the 7-year tribulation, and the 1,000-year millennium on earth.

Conclusion
God used Daniel to influence the political leadership of his day. Here was a Jewish boy who determined to live for God and ended up advising the greatest Gentile kings of his time. The Babylonians, like the Egyptians, placed great significance on the interpretation of dreams. They also honored wisdom,

science, and academic knowledge. It was in this environment that God raised up the brilliant Prophet Daniel as His spokesman. Daniel was a man with a message from heaven. He did not attempt to please the political or ecclesiastical monarchs of his day.

The story of Daniel's life ends with this statement: "So this Daniel prospered in the reign of Darius, and in the reign of Cyrus the Persian" (Dan. 6:28). Even though Daniel was a successful man, he was humble. He had every reason to become proud and arrogant, but he never did. He also had every reason to disassociate himself from his Jewish religious heritage, but he never did that either. Throughout his life, he remained faithful to the principles that made him great. A great champion of God never loses his grasp of this truth.

Daniel was also a man of wisdom. He was wise beyond his years as a teenager. He was a true spiritual and intellectual man. He shows us that both qualities are possible within the same person. One need not be a mental dummy in order to be spiritual. Nor does intelligence extinguish spirituality.

Ultimately, Daniel was a man of dependability and character. He was kind, courageous, committed, and victorious. A man's greatness is not determined by his talent, but by what it takes to discourage him. Daniel rose above his own enslavement in Babylon and stood up for God in that great city.

You too must decide once and for all whom you wish to please—God or the world. You cannot please both.

EIGHT
NEHEMIAH, THE BUILDER

NAME: Nehemiah, "Jehovah hath consoled"
DATES: Birth unknown; served as governor
of Judah from 445—415 B.C.
CHARACTER QUALITY: Determination
SIGNIFICANCE: Rebuilt Jerusalem's walls
in 445 B.C.; served as the cupbearer
to Persian King Artaxerxes I
KEY TEXT: Nehemiah 2:1-10

NEHEMIAH was determined to rebuild the city of Jerusalem after the Babylonian captivity. He totally dedicated himself to the protection and preservation of his people. His "call to the wall" literally preserved the messianic line of Christ.

Nehemiah was driven by his determination to fulfill God's call in his life. Because of his total commitment to his task, future generations of Israel enjoyed the blessing and protection of God. We too, like Nehemiah, must be determined to protect our generation for the sake of our children and grandchildren who will follow us. That is why I am determined to cry out against the sins of this generation and rebuild the walls of decency and morality. We must protect the next generation from the onslaught of Satan.

Cupbearer to the King

Nehemiah held the position of royal butler or cupbearer to King Artaxerxes, who ruled Persia from 465 to 424 B.C. Since the cupbearer worked very closely with the king, only a highly capable and trusted person would be given such a position. It was in the middle of the reign of Artaxerxes that

Nehemiah made his request to return to Jerusalem.

In 446 B.C. the walls of Jerusalem were destroyed. When the news of this terrible event reached Nehemiah, he "sat down and wept, and mourned certain days, and fasted, and prayed before the God of heaven" (Neh. 1:14). In 445 B.C. the Jews who had remained in Babylon and Persia became aware of the terrible conditions which existed in their beloved homeland. Upon hearing the tragic news of what had befallen his people and their city, Nehemiah determined that he would ask the king to commission him to personally gather the materials and lead the reconstruction of Jerusalem's walls. In April of 445 B.C., after praying for nearly four months, Nehemiah said to King Artaxerxes, "If it please the king, and if thy servant have found favor in thy sight, that thou wouldest send me unto Judah, unto the city of my fathers' sepulchers, that I may build it" (2:5).

Artaxerxes agreed to the request and not only commissioned Nehemiah to do the building, but equipped him with the material necessary to carry out the project (2:8). The king ordered material for the construction of the walls and provided official letters sanctioning the project (v. 9). Orders were sent to the governors beyond "the river" (Euphrates) to cooperate with Nehemiah in this matter. However, when Nehemiah arrived, he faced opposition from Sanballat, Tobiah, and Geshem (vv. 10, 19). There have always been and always will be those wretched people who oppose every work for God. Do not expect to be able to serve God without opposition. When you attempt great things for God, you must be prepared for great opposition.

Builder in Judah

Upon his arrival in Jerusalem, Nehemiah went out secretly at night to view the damaged walls and gates of the city.

> And I went out by night by the gate of the valley,
>   even before the dragon well, and to the dung port,

and viewed the walls of Jerusalem, which were
broken down, and the gates thereof were consumed with fire. Then I went on to the gate of the
fountain, and to the king's pool; but there was no
place for the beast that was under me to pass. Then
I went up in the night by the brook, and viewed
the wall, and turned back, and entered by the gate
of the valley, and so returned (Neh. 2:13-15).

Overwhelmed by what he saw, Nehemiah returned and
announced his intention to the Jewish leaders with these
words: " 'Ye see the distress that we are in, how Jerusalem
lieth waste, and the gates thereof are burned with fire; come,
and let us build up the wall of Jerusalem, that we be no more
a reproach.' Then I told them of the hand of my God which
was good upon me; as also the king's words that he had
spoken to me" (vv. 17-18).

The leaders were so thrilled with Nehemiah's commitment
and the official sanction of the Persian Emperor that they
immediately responded, "Let us rise up and build" (v. 18).

The project was led by Nehemiah who rallied together the
princes, priests, and people to work in one accord to build the
walls for both protection from invaders and for separation of
the Jews from the surrounding pagan peoples. The wall was to
serve as a protective hedge about the people of Jerusalem.
The various gates mentioned in the building project included:

Sheep Gate (3:1)	Fountain Gate (3:15)
Fish Gate (3:3)	Water Gate (3:26)
Old Gate (3:6)	Horse Gate (3:28)
Valley Gate (3:13)	East Gate (3:29)
Dung Gate (3:14)	Miphkad (Inspection) Gate (3:39)

Defending the Wall

Any significant work for God will always be met by both
human and satanic opposition. These combined forces did

their best to halt the rebuilding of the Jerusalem wall. Sanballat led this opposition against the Jews. "When Sanballat, and Tobiah, and the Arabians, and the Ammonites, and the Ashdodites, heard that the walls of Jerusalem were made up, and that the breaches began to be stopped, then they were very wroth, and conspired all of them together to come and to fight against Jerusalem, and to hinder it" (4:7-8).

Sanballat and the other members of the opposition tried many different tactics to prevent the reconstruction project:

RIDICULE	"They laughed us to scorn" (2:19).
CONSPIRACY	"They . . . conspired all of them together to come and fight against Jerusalem, and to hinder it" (4:7-8).
COMPROMISE	"Come, let us meet together" (6:2).
SLANDER	"Thou and the Jews think to rebel" (6:5).

On top of the external opposition that he faced, Nehemiah also had to deal with internal strife as well (3:5; 5:1-5). The laziness of the Tekoites and the extortion attempts of the wealthy Jews both had to be met with equal fervor. In spite of these problems, the city wall was finished in record time—just 52 days! (6:15)

Every church involved in a building project can learn great lessons from the problems Nehemiah encountered. Nehemiah was a great man, not because he was a great builder, but because he would not allow himself to be discouraged in his attempt to work for God.

Having rebuilt the wall, Nehemiah became determined to help repopulate the city. He set about a reclamation process to regather those that had returned earlier.

> And my God put into mine heart to gather
> together the nobles, and the rulers, and the peo-
> ple, that they might be reckoned by genealogy.
> And I found a register of the genealogy of them
> which came up at the first, and found written
> therein, "These are the children of the province,
> carried away, whom Nebuchadnezzar the king of
> Babylon had carried away, and came again to Jeru-
> salem and to Judah, every one unto his city" (7:5-
> 6).

Nehemiah was a man of great character. He set an unselfish example for the people by taking no salary during his first
12 years as governor (5:14). In fact, he paid for the food
consumed by his helpers (v. 17). He even worked hard on the
wall himself! (v. 16) He also displayed an unlimited confidence in God, understanding that the "joy of the Lord is your
strength" (8:10).

Nehemiah unconditionally refused to compromise and reminded his opponents that "the God of heaven He will
prosper us; therefore, we, His servants will arise and build"
(2:20). Nehemiah was a man of complete spiritual commitment. He remained steadfast against every attempted trick of
compromise and continued to pray day and night (4:9). He
even urged the men to build with their swords in one hand
and trowels in the other (4:17). Even his enemies "perceived
that this work was wrought of our God" (6:15-16). Nehemiah
was a testimony to his enemies as well as to his own people.

Revival at the Water Gate

Nehemiah was not only interested in the physical well-being
of the Children of Israel, but also in their spiritual well-being.
In Nehemiah 8 we have the record of the famous water gate
revival, which was led by Ezra and Nehemiah. (Nehemiah
was a younger contemporary of Ezra the priest, who had
journeyed back to Jerusalem in 458 B.C.)

During this revival, proper provisions were made for the reading of the Word of God and the preaching of the Word of God. Ezra stood on a "pulpit of wood" (8:4) so that the people could see him. Ezra and the Levites who were with him "read in the book in the law of God distinctly, and gave the sense, and caused [the people] to understand the reading" (v. 8).

The people responded by shouting, " 'Amen, Amen,' with lifting up their hands; and they bowed their heads, and worshiped the Lord with their faces to the ground. . . . All the people wept, when they heard the words of the Law" (vv. 6, 9).

As the people were confronted with the Law, they realized how they had sinned and they openly began to weep. In spite of the leaders' attempts to get them not to sorrow, the people were, nevertheless, overcome with grief.

Finally, the great revival resulted in the observation of the Feast of Tabernacles. Throughout the feast, the priests continued to read from the Book of the Law and the people continually wept before the Lord for seven days. On the eighth day, they assembled with fasting, in sackcloth, and with dust on their heads (9:1).

The commitment of the people to the Lord was so intense that they read the Word of God for one-fourth of the day and confessed their sins and worshiped the Lord another one-fourth of the day (9:3). In other words, they spent half of every day in the worship of God. They were so thankful that the Lord had delivered them from the Babylonian captivity and now had provided the protection of a wall around their city, that they poured out their hearts in rejoicing to the Lord.

The wall was finally dedicated with a great celebration as the people rejoiced and offered great sacrifices to the Lord (12:27-43). The Temple had already been rebuilt in 516 B.C. and the people renewed their commitment to worship the Lord in the newly consecrated edifice.

Nehemiah brought about such great reforms in Judah that the people who returned from the Babylonian captivity never again returned to the sin of idolatry which had sent them into captivity in the first place. Larger storerooms than ever had to be built in order to accommodate the tremendous offerings that the people were giving in the Temple during this period.

In the meantime, Nehemiah apparently returned to Babylon for some time in the service of King Artaxerxes. He later obtained a second leave and was able to return to Jerusalem again to oversee the work personally (13:6). Though he was originally concerned with the building of the wall, Nehemiah returned to demand that the House of God not be forsaken and that the proper arrangements be made for sacrifices, feasts, Sabbaths, and the proper worship of the Lord. Nehemiah even made civil reforms in order to maintain the sanctity of the people of God from their pagan neighbors. He was concerned about every facet of the spiritual, moral, civil, and political life of his people.

Conclusion

Nehemiah was a champion because he was a consecrated man of God. While we are most impressed with his commitment to the building of the walls of Jerusalem, we cannot overlook the fact that he was also committed to the rebuilding of the people of God. He realized that a nation's greatness was dependent upon the determination of its population to serve the Lord. Thus, he realized the promise of Scripture, "Blessed is that nation whose God is the Lord" (Ps. 33:12). Nehemiah was a great builder of people; thus, he was also a builder of a nation.

Nehemiah's story reminds us that material prosperity does not guarantee the blessing of God upon any people. A nation must be willing to submit both individually and corporately to God's authority in order to experience God's blessings. The hand of God was upon Nehemiah and as a result of his efforts, the nation of Judah was greatly blessed of God and the people were preserved in a time of adversity.

We too need leaders and champions like Nehemiah who are willing to stand up for God in a time when the walls and foundations of our society are being destroyed. The psalmist asks, "If the foundations be destroyed, what can the righteous do?" (Ps. 11:3). The foundation of America is its godly heritage from the past. If we allow that heritage to be destroyed by secularism and humanism, we too will find our nation destroyed.

There are many gates and walls broken down in the fabric of American society today. We must be willing to rebuild the moral foundation of our society at all costs. We face great opposition from those who decry and scorn the work of God in our society, but we must serve the Lord in spite of their scoffing.

When God burdened Nehemiah's heart for his people and their beloved city, he forsook all to obey God. Like a true champion, Nehemiah did not allow discouragement, trickery, ridicule, or internal strife to divert him from his goal. He never compromised—and neither should we!

NINE
ESTHER, THE QUEEN

NAME: Esther, "star"; Hadassah, "myrtle"
DATES: Became queen of Persia in 478 B.C.
CHARACTER QUALITY: Sacrifice
SIGNIFICANCE: Jewish orphan who became
    the wife of Ahasuerus (Xerxes),
    the Persian king; used by God to spare
    the entire Jewish race.
KEY TEXT: Esther 4:13-17

IN the Books of Ezra and Nehemiah we have the story of what happened to the minority of the Jewish people who returned to Jerusalem at the end of the Babylonian Captivity. But the Book of Esther describes what happened to the majority of the Jews who remained behind. The setting of this book is the ancient Persian Empire, which is the modern nation of Iran. Descendants of the Jews still live in Iran, though many have recently been persecuted by the Ayatollah Khomeini.

The suspense element in this story surrounds the first attempted holocaust of the Jewish people, which was narrowly averted by Esther's bold intervention. The villain, Haman the Agagite, was the Adolf Hitler of the Old Testament. Haman's subsequent hanging offers vivid fulfillment of Genesis 12:3: "And I will . . . curse him that curseth thee."

Interestingly, the name of God is never mentioned in the Book of Esther, though God's providential care is evident throughout this book. God was working behind the scenes to protect His people. It is possible that the book was deliberately written in this fashion to make it more accessible to the Jewish people who were living in the Dispersion.

Haman's initial attempt to exterminate the Jews posed the

worst threat ever to the messianic line. However, God was committed to preserving that line. God delights to take the worst of circumstances and from them produce the best results. Such was certainly the case with Esther and her people.

Esther's Rise

After several months of celebrating his rise to the throne, the Persian king Ahasuerus (Xerxes) ordered his wife Vashti to appear before his drunken friends.

> When the heart of the king was merry with wine, he commanded . . . the seven chamberlains that served in the presence of Ahasuerus the king, to bring Vashti the queen before the king with the crown royal, to show the people and princes her beauty; for she was fair to look on. But the queen Vashti refused to come at the king's commandment by his chamberlains; therefore was the king very wroth, and his anger burned in him (Esther 1:10-12).

When Vashti refused to obey the king's command, Ahasuerus bitterly deposed her from her throne and banished her from the empire (vv. 15-22). Now, minus a queen, he responded on the advice of his friends to conduct an empire-wide beauty contest in order to select another woman to become his wife and the new Queen of Persia. In the providence of God, a Jewish girl named Esther won that contest.

> So Esther was taken unto king Ahasuerus into his house royal. . . . And the king loved Esther above all the women, and she obtained grace and favor in his sight more than all the virgins; so that he set the royal crown upon her head, and made her queen instead of Vashti (2:16-17).

Esther had been raised by her older cousin Mordecai (vv. 5-7). When she was selected to be the new queen, she did not reveal her racial identity to Ahasuerus (v. 20). Esther's initial compromise was later transformed into ὲ ͻrilliant and noble confrontation with the enemies of her people.

Haman's Lies

Soon after Esther became queen, Ahasuerus appointed Haman to be his prime minister.

> After these things did King Ahasuerus promote Haman . . . and set him above all the princes that were with him. And all the king's servants, that were in the king's gate, bowed, and reverenced Haman; for the king had so commanded concerning him. But Mordecai bowed not, nor did him reverence (3:1-2).

Mordecai, in accord with his Jewish beliefs, refused to bow down to Haman. This angered Haman so much that he was "full of wrath" (v. 5). Realizing that Mordecai was a Jew, Haman plotted to exterminate not only Mordecai, but every other Jew living in the Persian Empire.

To make his plan legal, Haman went before King Ahasuerus to get his approval for the evil plot. He told the king:

> There is a certain people . . . in all the provinces of thy kingdom; and their laws are diverse from all people; neither keep they the king's laws; therefore it is not for the king's profit to suffer them. If it please the king, let it be written that they may be destroyed; and I will pay 10,000 talents of silver to the hands of those that have the charge of the business, to bring it into the king's treasuries (vv. 8-9).

Ahasuerus sanctioned Haman's scheme and said, "Do with [the people] as it seemeth good to thee" (v. 11).

Upon learning of this, Mordecai "rent his clothes, and put on sackcloth with ashes, and went out into the midst of the city, and cried with a loud and bitter cry" (4:1).

Word of Mordecai's actions got back to Queen Esther and she was "exceedingly grieved" (v. 4). She sent Hatach, her chamberlain, out to locate Mordecai and to find out why he was in mourning. "Mordecai told him all that had happened. . . . Also he gave him a copy of the writing of the decree . . . to show it unto Esther" (vv. 7-8).

Mordecai told Esther that if the mass murder took place, she would not escape just because she was in the king's house. He also reminded her that if she would not deliver her people, then deliverance would arise for the Jews from another source:

> For if thou altogether holdest thy peace at this time, then shall there enlargement and deliverance arise to the Jews from another place; but thou and thy father's house shall be destroyed; and who knoweth whether thou art come to the kingdom for such a time as this? (v. 14)

This is the great key to the entire Book of Esther. Esther was the right woman in the right place at the right time. She was the human instrument God used to change the course of history and preserve the line of the Messiah.

Esther's Boldness

In the ancient Persian Empire, a person could only approach the king's throne if he or she were asked to do so. To appear uninvited before the king was to invite the penalty of immediate death. Only if the king extended his scepter could the guest find favor in the king's sight and be properly received. Esther literally put her life on the line by going unannounced into the king's presence. With resolve of character and boldness, Esther determined, "If I perish, I perish" (4:16).

To Esther's great relief, she was warmly received by her husband. When he saw her standing in the outer court robed in her royal garments, he held out the golden scepter and she drew near, approaching cautiously, and reached out and

98 CHAMPIONS FOR GOD

touched the top of the scepter. The king told her that he
would grant her request, even up to half of the kingdom (5:1-
3).

Esther's initial request was quite simple. She asked that
both the king and Haman attend a special banquet which she
was preparing (v. 5).

After the banquet, Haman went forth "joyful and with a
glad heart; but when Haman saw Mordecai in the king's gate,
that he stood not up, nor moved for him, he was full of
indignation against Mordecai" (v. 9).

Mordecai's refusal to bow down before Haman stirred the
fire of hatred in Haman's heart. His wife and his friends didn't
want Haman to be upset when he attended the second royal
banquet the next evening. So they advised that a gallows be
built "that Mordecai may be hanged thereon; then go thou in
merrily with the king unto the banquet.' And the thing
pleased Haman; and he caused the gallows to be made" (v.
14).

But the night before the next banquet, the king suffered a
severe case of insomnia. He requested that some of the
historical records, the chronicles of the kings of Persia, be
read to him in order to put him to sleep. The records told of
how Mordecai had once saved the king's life by exposing an
assassination plot. The king asked how Mordecai had been
honored for his deed and discovered that nothing had been
done.

At that very moment, Haman arrived at the palace seeking
the king's permission to hang Mordecai. The king, determined to reward Mordecai, used Haman as a "sounding
board" and asked him, "What shall be done for the man
whom the king delighteth to honor?" (v. 6)

The self-centered Haman thought the king intended to
reward *him*, so he suggested:

> Let the royal apparel be brought which the king
> useth to wear, and the horse that the king rideth
> upon, and the crown royal which is set upon his

head; and let this apparel and horse be delivered to
the hand of one of the king's most noble princes,
that they may array the man withal whom the king
delighteth to honor, and bring him on horseback
through the street of the city, and proclaim before
him, "Thus shall it be done to the man whom the
king delighteth to honor" (vv. 8-9).

The king agreed with Haman's advice and ordered *him* to
perform all these deeds for *Mordecai!* (v. 10)

Having been totally humiliated, Haman returned home in
mourning (v. 12). His wife and his friends advised Haman,
"If Mordecai be of the seed of the Jews, before whom thou
hast begun to fall, thou shalt not prevail against him, but
shalt surely fall before him" (v. 13). While they were advising
him, the king's servant came to take Haman to the second
royal banquet.

During this banquet, Esther told her husband that there
was a plot underway to assassinate her and to slaughter all her
people. The king, filled with astonishment and anger, asked
her what terrible person intended to do this. She replied,
"The adversary and enemy is Haman" (7:6).

Ahasuerus was so angry that he was unable to speak and in
fury stormed out of the palace momentarily. In panic, Haman
threw himself upon Esther and begged for mercy. But when
the king returned, he interpreted Haman's action as an attempted assault upon his wife (vv. 7-8). Learning of the
nearby gallows which Haman had built for Mordecai, the
king ordered Haman himself to be hung from those gallows
that very night! (v. 10)

Mordecai's Prize

After the execution of Haman, Ahasuerus gave Haman's
estate to Esther and appointed her cousin Mordecai as his new
prime minister (8:1-2). The king also issued a counter decree
eliminating Haman's earlier attempt to have the Jews exter-

minated. As a result of all this "many of the people of the land became Jews" (v. 17)—that is, they became converts to the God Jehovah. Eight hundred of their enemies were killed in Shusan (9:6, 15) and over 75,000 were killed throughout the whole empire (v. 16).

To celebrate this wonderful deliverance and their victory over their enemies, Mordecai and Esther instituted a new memorial feast for the Jewish community, which is annually observed as the Feast of Purim. The term comes from the word *Pur*, which means to cast lots. Haman had done this in preparation to destroy the Jews (3:7), but Esther's brave determination had reversed it all. To this day, the Jewish people still celebrate the Feast of Purim. It is a time of remembering God's promise to vindicate the Jews against all of their enemies.

Mordecai's final promotion made him second only to King Ahasuerus (10:3). Mordecai dedicated his life to public service and to "seeking the wealth of his people, and speaking peace to all his seed" (v. 3).

Conclusion

Esther was one of God's champions because she risked her own life for the safety of her people. She put her own personal convenience on the altar of sacrifice in order to save the Jews. She was the human instrument which God used to bring about a great and glorious deliverance of His people.

While the name of God does not appear in the story of Esther, it is obvious that Esther had placed her confidence in God and not in fate. She was convinced that fasting and praying would bring about God's blessing on her endeavors (4:16). In Esther, we see the example of a beautiful girl who was willing to surrender her power and success for the sake of others. She responded in humility, rather than pride, and God blessed her for it. Esther was a true champion of God who put Him first.

TEN
JOHN, THE BAPTIST

NAME: John, "given of God"; "Baptist"
means that he practiced the rite of baptism
DATE: 6 B.C.—A.D. 29
CHARACTER QUALITY: Humility
SIGNIFICANCE: Forerunner of Christ;
baptized Jesus in the Jordan River to
initiate His public ministry
KEY TEXT: Matthew 3:1-17

JOHN'S humility and absolute devotion to Christ made him a champion of God. In confirming his humility, John himself announced, "[Christ] must increase, but I must decrease" (John 3:30). He lived a sacrificial life with the single purpose of preparing the Jews for the coming of the Messiah. He preached repentance and he baptized those who truly repented. It was his supreme privilege to introduce Christ to the world. What an honor!

John the Baptist was a transitional figure who signalled the end of the Old Testament era. In a verse that points to John's greatness and to his transitional status, Jesus said, "Verily I say unto you, among them that are born of women there hath not risen a greater than John the Baptist; notwithstanding he that is least in the kingdom of heaven is greater than he" (Matt. 11:11).

John the Baptist was unique in every way. He was bold in his stand and yet humble in his character. God has made each of us a unique individual, and He will greatly use each of us if we use our individuality to glorify Him. None of us will be exactly like John the Baptist. But like John, we must be who God intended us to be, whatever the cost.

By the world's standards, John was a failure. He lived in poverty in the wilderness. His disciples left him to follow Jesus and he was finally beheaded in prison. However, when the books of God are opened and all the world is judged, John will emerge as one of God's greatest champions.

The Birth of John

The story of John the Baptist begins before his birth. His father was a priest named Zacharias and his mother was Elisabeth. She was the cousin of Mary, the mother of Jesus. This elderly, righteous couple was childless. "And they were both righteous before God, walking in all the commandments and ordinances of the Lord blameless. And they had no child, because that Elisabeth was barren, and they both were now well stricken in years" (Luke 1:6-7).

Having no children was considered a disgrace in ancient Israel. But it had been the constant prayer of Zacharias that God might bless him with a child. However, because of their advanced ages, he and his wife had virtually given up all hope that it would ever become a reality. But one day while Zacharias was burning incense in the temple as part of his priestly duties, something very unusual happened. An angel of the Lord appeared to him and announced that his prayers had been answered—his wife would have a son, whose name was to be John. As if having a son at their age wasn't miraculous enough, the angel added: "For he shall be great in the sight of the Lord, and shall drink neither wine nor strong drink; and he shall be filled with the Holy Ghost, even from his mother's womb. And many of the Children of Israel shall he turn to the Lord their God" (vv. 15-16).

In the days of the Old Testament prophets, it had been prophesied that Elijah would one day return to the people of Israel (Mal. 4:5-6). When the angel appeared to Zacharias, he told him that his son John would come in the "spirit and power of Elias" (Luke 1:17). Jesus would later clearly state that the prophecy of the coming of Elijah had been fulfilled in the appearance of John the Baptist (Matt. 11:13-14)—though John himself made it clear that he was not literally Elijah (John 1:21).

Zacharias was so overcome by the angel's announcement that he could hardly believe it and questioned how it might be so. The angel recognized Zacharias' lack of faith and chastised him:

> And Zacharias said unto the angel, "Whereby shall I know this? For I am an old man, and my wife well stricken in years."

> And the angel answering said unto him, "I am Gabriel, that stand in the presence of God; and am sent to speak unto thee, and to show thee these glad tidings. And behold, thou shalt be dumb, and not able to speak, until the day that these things shall be performed, because thou believest not my words, which shall be fulfilled in their season" (Luke 1:18-20).

Elisabeth really did become pregnant, for which she was thankful to God (vv. 24-25). When the child finally arrived, the neighbors and relatives wanted to name the baby after his father, Zacharias. But the old priest, still unable to speak, wrote a note saying, "His name is John" (v. 63). Immediately thereafter, Zacharias' ability to speak returned. He praised the Lord and prophesied concerning the ministry of his child.

> And thou, child, shalt be called the prophet of the Highest; for thou shalt go before the face of the Lord to prepare His ways; to give knowledge of salvation unto His people by the remission of their sins, through the tender mercy of our God; whereby the dayspring from on high hath visited us, to give light to them that sit in darkness and in the shadow of death, to guide our feet into the way of peace (vv. 76-79).

The initial story of John's birth is followed by the statement: "And the child grew, and waxed strong in spirit, and was in the deserts till the day of his showing unto Israel" (v. 80). We are never told how it was that John ended up living in the desert, though it is logical to assume that his elderly parents probably died while he was still quite young. John, thus, grew up in the barren and remote region just north of the Dead Sea.

It has often been pointed out by scholars that John's ministry was conducted not far from the ancient settlement of Qumran, where the Essenes practiced the rite of baptism. While it is true that there was a close proximity of John's ministry to this location, this in no way means that John the Baptist was merely an Essene. There were many radical independent and divergent religious groups in Israel during the first century A.D. Scripture makes it clear that John's ministry was that of a singular individual, and not the product of a group or a community of leaders.

Prophetic Ministry

Because of the restriction against his drinking neither wine nor strong drink (Luke 1:15), and because of his generally restrictive lifestyle, it is sometimes assumed that John the Baptist was a Nazarite. It should be noted that Jesus was called a Nazarene, which simply meant that He was from the city of Nazareth. Being a Nazarene had to do with one's *location*, whereas being a Nazarite had to do with one's *vocation*. Jesus referred to differences between His lifestyle and John's when He noted that the religious leaders of Israel not only objected to John's stern lifestyle, but also objected to Jesus' frequent socializing with sinners in order to reach them (7:33-34).

Like Elijah of old, John was a rough and probably crude individual. He dressed in camel's hair, with a leather belt around his waist. The Bible says that his food was locusts and wild honey (Matt. 3:4). He was the New Testament version of Elijah.

The Apostle John describes John the Baptist as a "witness of the Light."

> There was a man sent from God, whose name was John. The same came for a witness, to bear witness of the Light, that all men through him might believe. He was not that Light, but was sent to bear witness of that Light (John 1:6-8).

When asked by the priests and Levites of Jerusalem who he was, John the Baptist clearly affirmed that he was not the Christ (John 1:20). Rather, he said of himself, "I am the voice of one crying in the wilderness" (v. 23).

There can be no doubt about the content of John's preaching. He came to call the nation of Israel to genuine spiritual repentance as a preparation for the coming of Jesus the Messiah. Thus, he loudly roared: "Repent ye; for the kingdom of heaven is at hand!" (Matt. 3:2)

Such stark ministry had not been known in Israel for centuries. Thus, multitudes of Jews from Judea and the Jordan valley flocked to hear him. But when the Pharisees and the Sadducees attempted to submit themselves to John's baptism, he denounced them as "vipers" (Matt. 3:7). He demanded that they show fruits worthy of repentance (v. 8). John reminded them that their physical descendancy from Abraham gave them no special privileges. God expected every person who believed in Him to produce fruit, just as one would expect a tree to bear fruit. Thus, John warned his generation that those who did not repent would fall under the judgment of the One who was coming after him. "He will thoroughly purge His floor, and gather His wheat into the garner; but He will burn up the chaff with unquenchable fire" (v. 12).

John's ministry was one of intense confrontation with the spiritual indifference of the Jews. In ministering so, he hoped to prepare the people to receive their Messiah.

The Practice of Baptism

> Then went out to [John] Jerusalem, and all Judea,
> and all the region round about Jordan, and were
> baptized of him in Jordan, confessing their sins
> (Matt. 3:5-6).

Baptism was an Old Testament as well as a New Testament
practice. Scripture makes it clear that John's baptism was not
New Testament, church-age baptism. Many years later some
of John's early followers came to Ephesus and encountered the
preaching of the Apostle Paul (Acts 19:1-7). Apparently,
they had believed John's message, repented, and been baptized. However, they were totally unaware of the death and
resurrection of Christ and of the descent of the Holy Spirit.
When Paul asked them whether they had received the Holy
Spirit when they believed, they replied, "We have not so
much as heard whether there be any Holy Ghost" (Acts
19:2). Having clearly heard the Gospel, these former followers of John were then "baptized in the name of the Lord Jesus"
(v. 5).

These men were caught in a dispensational transition from
the Old Testament era to the New Testament era. They
believed the message of the last great prophet of the Old
Testament era, John the Baptist. However, they now had
encountered the Apostle Paul who was preaching the message
of the death and resurrection of Christ as the basis for
salvation. Having already believed the message of God that
they had heard, these former disciples of John the Baptist
immediately believed the entire New Testament truth and
were rebaptized in the Christian (New Testament) baptism.

Thus, there is no basis to the idea that John the Baptist was
the founder of the Baptist church! Jesus Himself said that
those who were of His kingdom were greater than John the
Baptist (Luke 7:28). Jesus stated that a greater prophet had
not arisen than John the Baptist, but since John lived and
died prior to the death and resurrection of Christ, he lived
under the Old Testament dispensation. Therefore, he is re-

ferred to in Scripture as the "friend of the bridegroom" (John 3:29). John himself said that his joy was fulfilled in realizing that "[Christ] must increase, but I must decrease" (John 3:30). These statements indicate that John the Baptist did not consider himself to be a part of the Bride of Christ. Nor did he consider himself to be the Bridegroom. Like all Old Testament believers, John stands as one of the attendants at the wedding ceremony where Christ takes His bride-to-be, the church.

What then was the significance of John's baptism? It was not for the purpose of salvation and it certainly was not a testimony to the death, burial, and resurrection of Christ who had not yet died nor had yet risen from the dead. It was an act of spiritual obedience to God which followed true heart repentance. "Then said Paul, 'John verily baptized with the baptism of repentance, saying unto the people, that they should believe on Him which should come after him, that is, on Christ Jesus' " (Acts 19:4).

Like New Testament baptism, John's baptism was symbolic. John's baptism symbolized the cleansing which one experiences when he repents of his sins. By contrast, New Testament baptism does not symbolize cleansing, but rather our identification with the death and resurrection of Christ. Christian baptism symbolizes that our salvation is in our identification with and confidence in Christ's redemption.

John's Promise—The Coming Messiah

Throughout John's preaching ministry, he made it clear that he was the herald of the coming Messiah. "John answered them, saying, 'I baptize with water; but there standeth one among you, whom ye know not; He it is, who coming after me is preferred before me, whose shoe's latchet I am not worthy to unloose' " (John 1:26-27).

When approached by Jesus, John openly announced Christ's identity.

The next day John seeth Jesus coming unto him,
and saith, "Behold the Lamb of God, which taketh
away the sin of the world. This is He of whom I
said, 'After me cometh a man which is preferred
before me; for He was before me' " (John 1:29-30).

With such a clear realization of Christ's supremacy, it is not
surprising that John was reluctant to baptize Jesus when He
came to him. "Then cometh Jesus . . . unto John, to be
baptized of him. But John forbade Him, saying, 'I have need
to be baptized of Thee, and comest Thou to me?' " (Matt.
3:13-14) But Jesus insisted that John baptize Him "to fulfill
all righteousness" (v. 15).

So John had the wonderful privilege of baptizing Jesus and
initiating His public ministry. It was on this occasion that the
Spirit of God descended upon Jesus and the voice of the
Father spoke from heaven saying, "This is My beloved Son,
in whom I am well pleased" (v. 17).

From a human standpoint, Jesus was approximately six
months younger than John, but John recognized that Jesus
was in fact the preexistent and eternal Son of God. Thus
John's testimony was, "And I saw, and bare record that this is
the Son of God" (John 1:34). He was so committed to Jesus
that he freely allowed two of his most devoted followers to
leave him and join with the Saviour to be His disciples.
Andrew was one of the two. The identity of the other is not
certain (vv. 35-40).

In John the Baptist we find one of the most unselfish and
fearless servants of God. Even when facing the tragedy of his
own death, he remained faithful to the Saviour whom he
loved.

John's Persecution and Execution

King Herod apparently arrested John because of pressure from
Herodias, his wife. Herod had married Herodias while she was
already married to his brother. John publicly denounced

Herod's marriage to Herodias. This greatly angered Herodias, and she determined to have John killed. But Herod didn't want John to be killed because he feared John and considered him to be a "just and holy man" (Mark 6:20). But Herod also "feared the multitude, because they counted [John] as a prophet" (Matt. 14:5).

Though Herod imprisoned John, he tried to protect the prophet from death and willingly listened to John preach. However, on Herod's birthday the king had a great celebration for his officers and leaders. Herodias' daughter Salome danced for them and pleased Herod so much that he promised with an oath to give her whatever she would ask.

To Herod's shock and dismay, Salome, having been prompted by her mother, asked for John the Baptist's head on a platter (Matt. 14:8). The king was deeply distressed because he didn't want to kill John, but he felt constrained by his oath and by the intense excitement of those who sat with him at the table. So he commanded that John be beheaded. Tragically, John was beheaded in prison because of the unrepentant anger of Herod's ungodly wife. When the head was brought on the platter, Salome gave it to her mother. Though John was physically dead, like his predecessor Elijah, he was gone to glory.

Conclusion

The New Testament presents John the Baptist as the forerunner of Christ. His imprisonment was the signal for the beginning of Jesus' Galilean ministry. According to Jesus, John was the promised Elijah of Malachi 4:5 who was to come and complete his ministry of restoration on the eve of the "great and dreadful day of the Lord" (Mark 9:13).

John was a true champion of God in several ways. First of all, he was a man of prayer. It is interesting to note that when Jesus' disciples said to Him, "Lord, teach us to pray," they added the statement, "as John also taught his disciples" (Luke

11:1). John therefore was not only a man of prayer himself, but one who set an example for others to follow.

John was also a man of great unselfishness and tremendous personal courage. He was willing to rebuke the religious leaders and the political leaders of his day. He stood up to the Pharisees and the Sadducees and denounced them as vipers; he also stood up to Herod and denounced him for his immorality. There can be no doubt that if John were alive today he would thunder out against the major sins of our society as well. His message was clear and unequivocal.

Perhaps most notably, John the Baptist was a man of humility. He was willing to see himself diminish so that Christ might be magnified. There are very few Christians alive today who would be willing to do that. Too many of us are more caught up in our own glory rather than in the glory of the One we are called to serve. When I think of John the Baptist, I think of those dear and beloved believers who are persecuted for their faith in Christ. They know the true cost of decrease so that Christ might increase.

Our lives are brief at best. If a man lives only with the things of this life in view, his expectations will perish with him. Like John the Baptist, we must learn that only what is done for Christ will last. Can we say with John, "[Christ] must increase, but I must decrease"? (John 3:30)

ELEVEN
PETER, THE PREACHER

NAME: Originally called Simon. He was also
    called Cephas (Aramaic for "rock") or Petros
    (Greek for "stone")
DATES: Uncertain, about 10 B.C.—A.D. 68
CHARACTER QUALITY: Dedication
SIGNIFICANCE: A converted fisherman;
    one of the inner circle of Jesus' disciples
    and the early leader of the Twelve Apostles
KEY TEXT: Luke 5:1-11

PETER was the most popular of all the disciples. His sanguine personality caused him to be liked by all. His impulsive manner caused him to do things the other disciples were too timid to try. Peter was the most outspoken of the Twelve. Impetuous and impulsive, he was usually talking when he should have been listening. Despite his many ups and downs, he served the Lord with true dedication.

The Fisherman
The first chronological appearance of Peter in the New Testament is recorded in the Gospel of John. Here Andrew, Simon Peter's brother, tells him, "We have found the Messiah" (John 1:41). Then Andrew brought Peter to Jesus (v. 42). Andrew, initially a disciple of John the Baptist, left him to follow Jesus and brought his brother Peter with him.

Upon His initial meeting with Peter, somewhere near the Jordan River, Jesus said, "Thou art Simon the son of Jonah; thou shalt be called Cephas" (v. 42), which was the standard Aramaic word meaning "a stone." Hence, the English name Peter was taken from the Greek word for stone which is *petros.* Obviously, Peter was with Jesus from the very beginning of His earthly ministry.

Peter was originally a native of Bethsaida, which is on the Sea of Galilee (v. 44). He was a partner with James and John in the fishing business (Luke 5:7). At least four of these early disciples were fellow acquaintances. Scripture also makes it clear that Peter was a married man (Mark 1:30; 1 Cor. 9:5), and that he owned a permanent home at Capernaum in Galilee. He spoke Aramaic with a strong Galilean accent (Mark 14:70) and was accustomed to frequent contact with Gentiles. However, he maintained a strict Hebrew mentality toward Jewish purity and separation from defilement with Gentiles.

Having initially been brought to Jesus by his brother Andrew, Peter was officially "called" in an incident that took place at the Sea of Galilee. Jesus borrowed Peter's boat and went out in the water in it. From there, He taught the multitudes that gathered on the shoreline (Luke 5:3). After He finished teaching the crowd of people, Jesus told Peter:

> "Launch out into the deep, and let down your nets for a draught."
>
> And Simon answering said unto Him, "Master, we have toiled all the night, and have taken nothing; nevertheless at Thy word I will let down the net."
>
> And when they had this done, they enclosed a great multitude of fishes; and their net broke. And they beckoned unto their partners, which were in the other ship, that they should come and help them. And they came, and filled both the ships, so that they began to sink (Luke 5:4-7).

Early in Peter's relationship with Jesus, we see his willingness to obey the Lord's every command. Peter and his fellow fishermen caught such an incredible number of fish that their nets broke. Peter recognized the incident as a miracle from God. He fell down at Jesus' feet and cried, "Depart from me;

for I am a sinful man, O Lord" (v. 8). However, Jesus responded, "Fear not; henceforth thou shalt catch men" (v. 10). Overwhelmed by this amazing display of Jesus' power, Peter and his friends immediately "forsook all, and followed Him" (v. 11).

The Disciple

Scripture is filled with ample testimony to Peter's impulsive devotion to Christ (Mark 14:29; Luke 5:8; John 21:7). Nowhere is this more clear than in the incident where Peter walked on the water. Upon hearing that John the Baptist had been beheaded, Jesus and His disciples had retired to a deserted place. However, a great multitude thronged after them and our Lord miraculously fed the crowd of 5,000 (Matt. 14:13-21).

> And they did all eat. . . . And they that had eaten were about 5,000 men, besides women and children. And straightway Jesus constrained His disciples to get into a ship, and to go before Him unto the other side, while He sent the multitudes away.
>
> And when He had sent the multitudes away, He went up into a mountain apart to pray; and when the evening was come, He was there alone. But the ship was now in the midst of the sea, tossed with waves, for the wind was contrary.
>
> And in the fourth watch of the night Jesus went unto them, walking on the sea. And when the disciples saw Him walking on the sea, they were troubled, saying, "It is a spirit"; and they cried out for fear.
>
> But straightway Jesus spoke unto them, saying, "Be of good cheer; it is I; be not afraid" (Matt. 14:20-27).

Peter impulsively responded, "Lord, if it is You, command me to come to You on the water" (v. 28). Jesus bid him to

come and Peter got down out of the boat and walked on the
water to go to Jesus. But within a few moments, Peter became
fearful of the boisterous wind. "Beginning to sink, he cried,
saying, 'Lord, save me' " (v. 30).

It is easy for us to criticize Peter for this almost foolhardy
attempt and to overlook the fact that for a few moments he
did something that no one else had ever done—he walked on
the water! For a few moments, Peter was able to do something
by faith that the other disciples never would do. This was all
part of God's preparation time in Peter's life. He had learned
earlier to forsake his nets and follow the Lord. Now he
forsook his confidence in the natural and placed his confidence in the supernatural.

This incident concluded with Jesus' rescue of Peter:

> Immediately Jesus stretched forth His hand, and
> caught [Peter], and said unto him, "O thou of little
> faith, wherefore didst thou doubt?"
>
> And when they were come into the ship, the
> wind ceased. Then they that were in the ship came
> and worshiped Him, saying, "Of a truth Thou art
> the Son of God" (vv. 31-33).

Peter's consecration to the Lord Jesus was so intense that
he often appeared foolish in his devotion. Twice he ended up
in the water and in the Garden of Gethsemane he cut off the
ear of the high priest's servant in an attempt to physically
defend Jesus from arrest. Peter went so far on one occasion as
to rebuke the Lord publicly in front of the rest of the disciples. However, we should not overlook the fact that Peter was
a man who loved the Lord and was committed to serving
Him.

At the most crucial point in His earthly ministry, Jesus
took His disciples far to the north to the region of Caesarea
Philippi and asked them, "Whom do men say that I the Son
of man am?" (Matt. 16:13). They answered that some believed the Lord was John the Baptist or Elijah or Jeremiah or
one of the other prophets come back from the dead (v. 14).

Then He asked them, "But whom say ye that I am?" (v. 15)

Peter, who usually served as the spokesman for the 12 disciples, said, "Thou art the Christ, the Son of the living God" (v. 16). His confession, which stands as being representative of the Twelve Apostles, affirms the Messiahship and deity of Christ simultaneously.

In response, Jesus answered:

> Blessed art thou, Simon Barjona; for flesh and blood hath not revealed it unto thee, but My Father which is in heaven. And I say unto thee, that thou art Peter, and upon this rock I will build My church; and the gates of hell shall not prevail against it. And I will give unto thee the keys of the kingdom of heaven, and whatsoever thou shalt bind on earth shall be bound in heaven; and whatsoever thou shalt loose on earth shall be loosed in heaven (16:17-19).

Jesus' statement about the foundation of the church has been greatly debated. Was He saying that He would build His church upon Peter or upon Peter's confession of faith? Attempts to distinguish between the use of Peter's name and the word *rock* are inconsequential and based on a misunderstanding of the vocative case underlying the Aramaic original. Protestant interpretation has traditionally understood that it is the confession of the deity and the messiahship of Christ which is the foundation of the church. First Corinthians 3:11 tells us that Christ Himself is the foundation of the church. Peter, representative of the Twelve Apostles, is, in a secondary sense, part of that foundation, as are all the apostles. Hence, the Book of Revelation symbolizes the Twelve Apostles in the twelve foundations of the New Jerusalem (Rev. 21:14).

The purpose of the church is stated as that of attacking the gates of hell. Jesus never saw the church as passively functioning within the world, but rather as aggressively confronting the gates of hell itself! Thus, He viewed the church on earth as the "church militant" and the church in heaven as the "church triumphant."

The Lord's reference to the giving of the "keys of the kingdom of heaven" is extended to all of the disciples and not limited to Peter. While Peter, again representing the apostles, first used the keys on the Day of Pentecost, all of the apostles became effective in the use of the keys of the kingdom—which refers to the preaching of the Gospel itself. Thus, men are bound or loosed by their response to the Gospel.

Peter's confession of faith was followed by an immediate mistake. In order to help His disciples understand what it would take to establish a church, Jesus explained to His disciples "how that He must go unto Jerusalem, and suffer many things of the elders and chief priests and scribes, and be killed, and be raised again the third day" (Matt. 16:21).

Peter took the Lord aside and rebuked Him, saying, "Be it far from Thee, Lord; this shall not be unto Thee" (v. 22). Jesus then turned to Peter and said, "Get thee behind Me, Satan!" (v. 23) Thus, within a matter of moments, Peter went from the height of honor with his confession of faith to the pit of disappointment with a public rebuke. Therefore, Jesus reminded His disciples that the real solution to their lives was to deny themselves and take up their crosses and follow Him (v. 24).

Six days after Peter's confession, Jesus took him, James, and John to a mountain where He "was transfigured before them; and His face did shine as the sun, and His raiment was white as light. And, behold, there appeared unto them Moses and Elias talking with Him" (17:2-3). The transfiguration was proof of Jesus' deity, which would be finally confirmed by His resurrection. At the height of this spiritual experience, Peter was sound asleep (Luke 9:32). He woke up and saw Moses representing the Law and Elijah representing the prophets, along with the Lord. Peter concluded, "Lord, it is good for us to be here; if Thou wilt, let us make here three tabernacles;

one for Thee, and one for Moses, and one for Elias" (Matt. 17:4). While Peter was still talking "a bright cloud overshadowed them; and behold a voice out of the cloud, which said, 'This is My beloved Son, in whom I am well pleased; hear ye Him.' And when the disciples heard it, they fell on their faces, and were sore afraid" (vv. 5-6).

This incident was eventually followed by the night of disaster when Jesus announced to His disciples that one of them would betray Him and all of them would forsake Him (26:31). Shocked at His prediction, Peter said, "Though all men shall be offended because of Thee, yet will I never be offended" (v. 33). Jesus then prophesied, that before the night was over, Peter would deny Him three times (v. 34).

Later that night when Jesus was arrested in the Garden of Gethsemane, Peter attempted to defend the Lord. "Then Simon Peter having a sword drew it, and smote the high priest's servant, and cut off his right ear. . . . Then said Jesus unto Peter, 'Put up thy sword into thy sheath; the cup which My Father hath given Me, shall I not drink it?' " (John 18:10-11) Then Jesus healed the servant by restoring his ear (Luke 22:51).

Apparently from this point on, Peter's personal hurt and bitterness that night became so great that he fell into an utter denial of Christ. Jesus was taken across the valley to the palace of the high priest and put on public trial, which Peter could see from the courtyard below (Matt. 26:58). There Peter was confronted three times by different individuals who asked him whether he was one of Jesus' disciples. Each time, Peter's denial grew stronger:

"I know not what thou sayest" (Matt. 26:70).
Again he denied with an oath, "I do not know the Man" (v. 72).
Then began he to curse and to swear, saying, "I know not the Man" (v. 74).
It was not the cock crowing which reminded Peter of

what he had done, but the fact that Jesus, at that very
moment, turned and looked at him (Luke 22:61). Broken-
hearted by his failure, Peter "went out and wept bitterly"
(Matt. 26:75). Peter was so utterly broken by his failure to
affirm the One he loved that he never appeared at the scene
of the crucifixion.

However, after the Lord's resurrection, Peter ran to the
tomb with John. Shocked that the body of the Lord was
missing, Peter even examined the graveclothes (Luke 24:12).
He was present eight nights later when Jesus appeared to the
disciples in the Upper Room (vv. 36-43). On each of these
occasions Peter was present, but there is no record of any
personal conversation between him and Jesus.

Peter's restoration occurs before our Lord's Ascension.
Some of the disciples were in Galilee and went fishing at
Peter's suggestion.

That night they caught nothing. But when the
morning was now come, Jesus stood on the shore;
but the disciples knew not that it was Jesus.

Then Jesus saith unto them, "Children, have ye
any meat?"

They answered Him, "No."

And He said unto them, "Cast the net on the
right side of the ship, and ye shall find."

They cast therefore, and now they were not able
to draw it for the multitude of fishes. Therefore
that disciple whom Jesus loved saith unto Peter, "It
is the Lord" (John 21:3-7).

When Peter realized that what John said was true, he was
so excited that he dove in the water and swam to shore (v. 7).
As he and the other disciples came to shore, "they saw a fire
of coals there, and fish laid thereon, and bread" (v. 9). Jesus
was cooking breakfast for them. He told them:

"Bring of the fish which ye have now caught."

Simon Peter went up, and drew the net to land
full of great fishes, an hundred and fifty and three;

and for all there were so many, yet was not the net broken.

Jesus saith unto them, "Come and dine."

And none of the disciples durst ask Him, 'Who art Thou?' knowing it was the Lord. Jesus then cometh, and taketh bread, and giveth them, and fish likewise (vv. 10-13).

After the meal, Jesus asked Peter three times if he loved Him. Each time, Peter affirmed that he did indeed love His Lord. Jesus then asked him to feed His sheep (vv. 15-17). Peter's three affirmations of love, which counterbalanced his three previous denials, restored him to the place of leadership and service to which he had been called. The command to "Feed My sheep" is in essence the Lord's call to go and serve.

The significance of this encounter was not the play on the use of terminology (sheep, lambs), but rather in the fact that the three affirmations countered Peter's three denials which had occurred earlier. At this time, Jesus predicted that Peter would eventually be martyred for his faith: "When thou wast young, thou girdest thyself, and walkedst whither thou wouldest; but when thou shalt be old, thou shalt stretch forth thy hands, and another shall gird thee, and carry thee whither thou wouldest not" (v. 18). The reference to the phrase "stretch forth thy hands" has been taken as a prediction of Peter's upside-down crucifixion which occurred many years later.

The Apostle

On the Day of Pentecost, 50 days after the Passover, the disciples were all together in one place "with one accord" (Acts 2:1). It was then that the Holy Spirit came upon them for the first time. They began to speak the Gospel (the Good News of the death, burial, and resurrection of Christ) in such a manner that they could be understood by various Jewish proselytes in their native languages and dialects. "There were dwelling at Jerusalem Jews, devout men, out of every nation under heaven. . . . Every man heard them speak in his own language" (vv. 5-6). This amazing miracle caused people to ask what all of this meant.

Peter, empowered by the Holy Spirit, stood up and preached the first sermon of the Church Age. Peter's sermon emphasized the person and work of Christ and His atonement on the cross. When the crowd responded, "What shall we do?" (v. 37), Peter told them, "Repent, and be baptized every one of you in the name of Jesus Christ for the remission of sins, and ye shall receive the gift of the Holy Ghost" (v. 38). Three thousand responded to that invitation and were baptized that same day! (v. 44) Peter may have had his ups and downs, but on that day he was God's spokesman to the nation of Israel.

There can be no doubt that Peter was the spokesman and leader of the apostles at this point. While he did not serve as the pastor of the Jerusalem church, he nevertheless was the leading spokesman of the disciples in the early days of the Church Age.

Sometime later, Peter and John went up to the temple to pray. At one of the temple gates, they saw a lame man who was begging for money. Peter said to him, "Silver and gold have I none, but such as I have give I unto thee; in the name of Jesus Christ of Nazareth rise up and walk" (Acts 3:6). Peter took the man by the hand and lifted him up. Immediately the man's feet and ankles were strengthened and he was miraculously healed (v. 7). The man not only stood up and walked, but he leaped up and went with them into the temple—walking, leaping, and praising God! (v. 8)

All of this attracted the attention of the crowd at Solomon's porch and gave Peter an opportunity to preach another sermon. This time his message was the same: "Repent ye therefore, and be converted, that your sins may be blotted out" (v. 19). Even though 5,000 trusted in Christ as Saviour (4:4), Peter and John were arrested for creating a disturbance in the temple area.

The Sanhedrin tried to prohibit Peter and John from preaching in the name of Jesus. But the disciples insisted, "Whether it be right in the sight of God to hearken unto you more than unto God, judge ye. For we cannot but speak the things which we have seen and heard" (Acts 4:19-20). After being threatened, Peter and John were released. They returned to the church to encourage the believers in their stand for Christ.

Later on, Peter was living in Joppa, on the coast of the Mediterranean Sea, when he received a vision from the Lord. Peter was told to rise and eat of the kinds of animals that he had always considered unclean according to the Mosaic Law (10:9-16). At that very moment, a delegation of Gentile guests arrived at Peter's house. They had been sent by Cornelius, a centurion of the Italian regiment of the Roman army, who was stationed in Caesarea, to the north. Peter accepted the invitation of the delegation and traveled with them to Caesarea to meet Cornelius. Peter told him, "Whosoever believeth in [Christ] shall receive remission of sins" (v. 43).

While Peter was still proclaiming the Gospel, the Holy Spirit fell on those who heard his words. While Peter was astonished that Gentiles would receive the Holy Spirit, he realized that their conversions were real. Thus, Peter asked, "Can any man forbid water, that these should not be baptized, which have received the Holy Ghost as well as we?" (v. 47) This opened the door of salvation to the Gentiles as Peter again used the keys of the Gospel to unlock the gates of hell and set people free.

Peter's place of ministry in the early church maintained a significant role for many years to follow, despite the rising influence of the Apostle Paul. While the Book of Acts shifts to cover Paul's life and mission, we should not assume that Peter paled into insignificance. Until his martyrdom, Peter was a major influence in the early church.

Conclusion

Peter was a great champion for God because he was a man of
dedication. There was certainly nothing supernatural about
Peter. He was definitely not infallible. In fact, he had to be
rebuked on several occasions by the Lord and even later by
the Apostle Paul (Gal. 1:11). Peter often spoke up without
thinking and acted without considering the consequences of
his actions. However, this mighty man of God was touched
by God's infinite grace.

Peter was a great preacher of Jesus Christ. His sermons in
the early days of the church were clearcut confessions of the
person and work of Christ and exhortations to salvation.
That Peter called his converts to repentance faith is clear.
There can be no true repentance without faith, and there can
be no true faith without repentance.

In dealing with us, God usually operates more slowly than
we do. If we are not careful, we will get ahead of God's
timetable for our lives. When we try to do ourselves what
God wants to do through us, we will always mess things up. It
took Peter most of his life to learn to wait on God. I admit it
has taken me just as long to learn it.

I have often said that the difference between mediocrity
and greatness is vision. With no vision, the people perish.
We must comprehend what God wants us to do and, by His
strength, make it become a reality. However, in all our
sincerity to fulfill that vision, we must be willing to wait on
God.

God wants you to be a champion, as Peter was. But a
champion must live by the rules. Peter learned that lesson the
hard way. The sooner you learn that lesson, the sooner you
will be ready to serve the Lord.

TWELVE
PAUL,
THE CHURCH-PLANTER

NAME: Saul, later changed to Greek Paulos, "small"
DATES: About A.D. 1—A.D. 68
CHARACTER QUALITY: Confidence
SIGNIFICANCE: Greatest missionary evangelist of
    all time; New Testament author,
    preacher, and church-planter
KEY TEXT: Acts 9:1-7

PAUL had the heart of a pastor, the mind of a scholar, the feet of a missionary, the drive of an evangelist, and the hide of an elephant! He wrote more than half of the books in the New Testament. He planted churches all over Europe and Asia. His message and motive were Christ and his manner was confident. In a dramatic encounter with God, he had met Christ on the road to Damascus. He knew the Bible, theology, and people. He was confident in the power of the Word of God. Certainly, he was one of God's greatest champions.

Paul suffered greatly for his faith in Christ. He was beaten, stoned, imprisoned, and shipwrecked. But he never gave up. His life was a miracle of God's grace. I am glad that when God forgives us, He puts our sins in the depth of the deepest sea, never to be remembered against us. When God forgives, He forgets—and so should we. Don't drag things out of the sea that God has put there and forgotten and forgiven. If you have accepted Christ as your Saviour, God has placed you in fellowship with His dear Son. Your first obligation is to know Him, love Him, walk with Him, fellowship with Him, and commune with Him.

Contempt for the Church

The Apostle Paul was born and raised in Tarsus in Asia Minor in the strictest Jewish manner (Acts 21:39). He was from the tribe of Benjamin and was both a Pharisee and the son of a Pharisee (Rom. 11:1; Acts 23:6). As a young man, he had studied under Gamaliel, one of the greatest Jewish teachers of the time (Acts 22:3). Paul was evidently about 30 years old when his public persecution of the early church began. He stated, "I persecuted this way to the death" (22:4).

Paul first appears in the New Testament as Saul, a young man consenting to the death of Stephen and holding the clothes of those who stoned him (7:58). Scripture never indicates what particular impact Stephen's martyrdom had on Saul, but it is reasonable to assume that he could not have watched the death of this godly man without being greatly affected by Stephen's confidence in the Lord.

After Stephen's death, Saul became the leader of the persecution against the church in Jerusalem (8:1). Saul was instrumental in scattering the early disciples throughout Judea and Samaria. He "made havoc of the church," entering into Christian homes and literally arresting men and women and committing them to prison (v. 3). In spite of his attempts to persecute the church, God used Saul's efforts to scatter the Christians throughout the Roman Empire—and they preached the Gospel of Christ's death and resurrection everywhere they went (v. 4). Paul later recounted his early experiences before the Jerusalem mob (chaps. 23—26). It was not something of which he was proud, but rather a means of showing the great change that Christ had brought in his life.

Conversion at Damascus

Saul "yet breathing out threatenings and slaughter against the disciples of the Lord," went to see the high priest in Jerusalem (Acts 9:1). He wanted the priest to give him an official letter, sanctioning his persecution of the Christians in the synagogues of Damascus, where there was a large Jewish settlement (v. 2).

On his way to Damascus, Saul was confronted by the resurrected Christ:

> Suddenly there shined round about [Saul] a light from heaven; and he fell to the earth, and heard a voice saying unto him, "Saul, Saul, why persecutest thou Me?"
>
> And he said, "Who art Thou, Lord?"
>
> And the Lord said, "I am Jesus whom thou persecutest; it is hard for thee to kick against the pricks."
>
> And he trembling and astonished said, "Lord, what wilt Thou have me to do?"
>
> And the Lord said unto him, "Arise, and go into the city, and it shall be told thee what thou must do."
>
> And the men which journeyed with him stood speechless, hearing a voice, but seeing no man. And Saul arose from the earth; and when his eyes were opened, he saw no man. . . .And he was three days without sight, and neither did eat nor drink (Acts 9:3-9).

When Saul got to Damascus, he was visited by a Christian named Ananias. This faithful man had been instructed by the Lord to put his hands on Saul and heal his blindness (vv. 12, 18). Though Ananias had been worried about Saul's reputation for persecuting Christians, God had assured him that he would not be harmed by Saul. The Lord told Ananias, "Go thy way; for [Saul] is a chosen vessel unto Me, to bear My name before the Gentiles, and kings, and the Children of Israel" (v. 15).

When Ananias arrived at the house where Saul was, he put his hands on Saul and said:

> "Brother Saul, the Lord, even Jesus, that appeared unto thee in the way as thou comest, hath sent

me, that thou mightest receive thy sight, and be
filled with the Holy Ghost."

And immediately there fell from his eyes as it
had been scales; and he received sight forthwith,
and arose, and was baptized (vv. 17-18).

Saul's conversion was so drastically unexpected that at first
Christians were reluctant to accept him into their fellowship.
He immediately began to preach Christ in the synagogues in
Damascus and affirmed that Jesus was in fact the Son of God
(v. 20). Saul's superior intelligence caused him to confound
those who would deny his claims, so they plotted to kill him
(vv. 22-24). He narrowly escaped by night, going over the
city wall in a large basket (v. 25).

Saul traveled straight to Jerusalem, where the apostles were
also reluctant to accept him. Then they heard him disputing
against the Hellenistic Jews, affirming his belief in Christ,
and the apostles had no more doubts that Saul's conversion
was genuine. As a result of Saul's conversion, the churches
had peace "throughout all Judea and Galilee and Samaria" (v.
31).

Little else is said of Saul's early life. We know that Paul
spent nearly two years in the Trans-Jordan desert, referred to
as "Arabia" (Gal. 1:17), and that he eventually returned to
his native Tarsus. After some 10 or 12 years, Barnabas requested that Saul (or Paul as he was also called, see Acts
13:9), come to Antioch in Syria to help minister in a Gentile
church there (Acts 9:26; 11:20). It was there that the believers were first called "Christians" (11:26). From Antioch, Paul
and Barnabas were sent on a "famine visit" (relief effort) to
help the poverty-stricken Christians in Jerusalem (vv. 27-30).
Upon their return in about A.D. 47, Paul and Barnabas were
commissioned by the church in Antioch to embark on an
evangelistic tour which would take them initially to Barnabas'
homeland of Cyprus.

It is important to note that Paul and Barnabas did not
decide merely to go on an evangelistic-missionary campaign

on their own. They were set apart by the church at Antioch, whose leaders laid their hands on them and commissioned them for their missionary activity (13:1-3). The importance of the local church throughout the New Testament is evident everywhere. There were no unattached believers wandering around ministering apart from local churches which were established throughout the Roman Empire. Thus, Paul did not become engaged in merely getting people to make decisions for Christ, but rather he organized his converts into local churches. Thus, his greatest work was that of a church-planter. Paul blazed virgin territory with the message of the Gospel, establishing some 50 churches throughout the Roman world. From those churches, the Gospel spread through Europe and eventually to the Western world.

First Journey: Cyprus & Asia Minor

Paul, Barnabas, and John Mark set sail for Cyprus where Paul used his Gentile name in order to be more effective in reaching Gentiles. He worked his first recorded miracle, the blinding of Elymas (Acts 13:8-11). Paul also won the deputy of Paphos, Sergius Paulus, to Christ (vv. 7, 12).

After successful evangelistic efforts in Cyprus, Paul and Barnabas sailed to Antioch in Pisidia on the southern coast of Asia Minor. Here Paul preached his first recorded sermon. He invited his listeners to receive the "forgiveness of sins" by believing in Christ's finished work on the cross and in His resurrection from the dead (vv. 38-39). Several Jews as well as Gentiles responded to his message and placed their faith in Christ (v. 43). However, the Jewish leaders rejected Paul's message and drove him out of town (vv. 45, 50).

From there, Paul and his company traveled to Iconium and many again believed the Gospel (13:51—14:1). At Lystra, Paul healed a crippled man who had never walked.

> There sat a certain man at Lystra, impotent in his
> feet, being a cripple from his mother's womb, who

never had walked; the same heard Paul speak; who steadfastly beholding him, and perceiving that he had faith to be healed, said with a loud voice, "Stand upright on thy feet." And he leaped and walked about.

And when the people saw what Paul had done, they lifted up their voices, saying . . ."The gods are come down to us in the likeness of men" (14:8-11).

But Paul and Barnabas refused the worship of the people and told them, "We also are men of like passions with you, and preach unto you that ye should turn from these vanities unto the living God" (v. 15).

The people, however, were still excited by the miracle. They wanted to offer sacrifices to Paul and Barnabas (v. 18). Then some Jews from Antioch and Iconium came and won the crowd over. The people of Lystra stoned Paul, and "drew him out of the city, supposing he had been dead" (v. 19). But Paul was supernaturally raised to life and went right back into Lystra and continued preaching (v. 20).

Having completed a successful tour in southern Galatia, Paul and Barnabas returned to Antioch in Syria in order to report on the results of their journey (vv. 26-28). The success of their mission to the Gentiles necessitated the Jerusalem Council (chap. 15), where the Apostles sanctioned further evangelistic efforts to the Gentiles.

Second Journey: Asia Minor & Macedonia

Paul's second missionary journey began with a dispute with Barnabas. Barnabas wanted John Mark, who had left them and returned home on the first journey, to accompany them on the second journey. However, Paul refused to take him along, and Barnabas and John Mark left for Cyprus (Acts 15:39). Paul took Silas with him (v. 40) and journeyed to Asia Minor, taking the overland route through Tarsus and on to Derbe and to Lystra, where Timothy joined them (16:1-3). Timothy had apparently been converted during Paul's preaching there on his first missionary journey.

From there they went to Troas where Paul received his Macedonian vision. "A vision appeared to Paul in the night. There stood a man of Macedonia, and prayed him, saying, 'Come over into Macedonia, and help us' " (16:9). Right away Paul and his team, which by now included the physician Luke, left Troas (v. 10). They crossed over into Europe and arrived at Philippi in Macedonia where Paul was involved in conversions of three people—a businesswoman named Lydia, a demoniac girl, and a prison keeper (vv. 11-40).

From there they journeyed to Thessalonica where Paul spent three weeks in the home of Jason (17:1-9). After opposition to the Gospel was stirred up in that city, Paul was warmly received by the devout Bible students at Berea (vv. 10-13). But persecution became so intense in Berea that Paul traveled alone to Athens (vv. 14-15).

While in Athens, Paul preached a sermon on Mars Hill about the "unknown god." His message emphasized God as the Creator, Saviour, and Judge of all things (vv. 22-31).

From Athens Paul traveled to Corinth where he was rejoined by Silas and Timothy. In Corinth Paul met Aquila and Priscilla, a devout Christian couple who were also tentmakers. Paul remained in Corinth for 18 months. While he was there, he wrote the letters which became the books of 1 and 2 Thessalonians (18:1-18). Paul eventually traveled to Ephesus for a brief time, accompanied by Aquila and Priscilla, who remained behind to encourage the church there (vv. 19-21). Finally, Paul returned again to Antioch in Syria to report to his home church the results of his evangelistic travels.

Third Journey: Asia Minor & Macedonia
On his third missionary journey, Paul traveled again from Antioch by land to Lystra and on to Ephesus where he spent

the major portion of his time, remaining there for nearly two years. Having traveled all over the region of Galatia and Phrygia (Acts 18:23), Paul concentrated his efforts in Ephesus. The church established there was to become the great mother church of Asia Minor (see Rev. 2:1-7). In Ephesus Paul influenced the ministry of Apollos who would later become the pastor of the church at Corinth (1 Cor. 3:6). Paul dealt with the disciples of John the Baptist who had not yet fully heard the Gospel (Acts 19:1-6). Paul ended up in a riotous confrontation with the devotees of the goddess Diana before he left Ephesus (vv. 24-41).

Paul then departed to Greece and spent three months there encouraging the disciples in the various churches (20:3). He eventually returned to Troas and reassembled his team, including Timothy and Luke. While they were at Troas, Paul preached a long sermon that lasted well into the night. A young man named Eutychus, who had fallen asleep as Paul preached, fell out of a third story balcony and landed on the floor, dead. Paul miraculously brought him back to life (vv. 8-12).

Paul then left for the seaport town of Miletus, where the Ephesian elders came out to meet him. Paul reviewed with them the essential elements of his message and ministry (vv. 19-30). He emphasized that his message was one of "testifying both to Jews, and also to Greeks, repentance toward God, and faith toward our Lord Jesus Christ" (v. 21). Paul and his team sailed to Tyre and down to Caesarea. They were received by Philip before Paul was warned by Agabus not to go to Jerusalem (chaps. 22—28).

Confinement in Prison

Caesarea. Against all human advice, and apparently under the direction of God, Paul deliberately returned to his beloved Jerusalem to pour out his heart of concern to his people. Instead of the reception he had hoped for, Paul was met by severe reprisal from Ananias the high priest (Acts 23:1-2). Paul was rescued by the Roman commander who removed him at night to Caesarea under the protection of 470 armed soldiers (vv. 10, 23-24).

For nearly two years Paul remained in prison in Caesarea where he testified to governors Felix (23:31—24:27) and Festus (25:1-12) as well as King Herod Agrippa II (25:13—26:32). To each of them, Paul emphasized that he was innocent of the charges against him and urged them to accept Christ themselves. Here we see the determination of this great champion of God who would not allow himself to be defeated nor discouraged in this time of human disappointment. Even in prison, he was still an instrument of God's grace.

Finally, Paul appealed his case to Caesar, emphasizing his Roman citizenship rights. Paul was sent from Caesarea to Rome under armed protection and on the way encountered a terrible shipwreck which resulted in a three-month delay on the island of Melita or Malta (27:14—28:10). Even during this delay, Paul was mightily used by God to reach Publius, the leading citizen of the island. Paul preached and healed many and helped establish the church on that island as well.

Rome. After a three-month delay, Paul was finally taken via the Appian Way to Rome, where he further conducted an effective ministry even reaching some of the people of Caesar's household. It was during this time that he wrote many of his most important New Testament letters—Ephesians, Colossians, Philippians, Philemon, 1 Timothy, Titus, and eventually 2 Timothy.

It is difficult to discern whether Paul was actually imprisoned for one long time in Rome or for two lesser periods. Many feel that his first Roman imprisonment was followed by a brief release, which in turn was followed by a second imprisonment, and finally by his death. Paul was beheaded in A.D. 68.

As the Book of Acts closes, Paul is ecstatic about his

opportunity to preach the Gospel to the Gentiles. He said, "Therefore let it be known to you that the salvation of God has been sent to the Gentiles, and they will hear it" (28:28).

Conclusion

Paul was a great champion because he was a man of prayer. When Ananias came seeking him in Damascus, he was told, "Behold he prayeth" (Acts 9:11). Paul began and ended his ministry with prayer (2 Tim. 4:16). Prayer is not conquering God's reluctance to answer, but laying hold of His willingness to help. Throughout my own ministry, prayer has motivated and sustained me.

Paul was an outstanding evangelist and soul-winner. Evangelism is the key to church growth. Growing churches are evangelistic churches. Ours is a soul-winning church. Our burden is to reach our community and the world for Christ in our lifetime.

Paul was also a great champion because he suffered cheerfully for the cause of Christ. When he was first converted, the Lord told Ananias: "I will show [Paul] how great things he must suffer for My namesake" (Acts 9:16). In Paul's lifetime, he was plotted against on at least six occasions. His work was constantly opposed by his own countrymen. He was stoned and left for dead once, suffered repeated beatings, endured four shipwrecks, was ridiculed by secular philosophers, suffered snakebite, and was finally left on death row—forsaken even by his closest friends.

The martyred missionary, Jim Elliot, summarized his own testimony as well as that of the Apostle Paul when he wrote, "He is no fool who gives what he cannot keep to gain what he cannot lose." Paul discovered this secret and confidently exclaimed:

> For to me to live is Christ,
> and to die is gain.
> (Philippians 1:21)